LECTIONARY FOR THE CHRISTIAN PEOPLE

LECTIONARY
FOR THE CHRISTIAN PEOPLE

Cycle B of the Roman,
Episcopal, Lutheran Lectionaries

Revised Standard Version texts
emended

PUEBLO PUBLISHING COMPANY
New York

FORTRESS PRESS
Philadelphia

Editors: Gordon Lathrop and Gail Ramshaw

Design: Frank Kacmarcik

The Scripture quotations contained herein are from
the Revised Standard Version Bible, copyright 1946,
1952, 1971 by the Division of Christian Education
of the National Council of the Churches of Christ
in the USA, and are used by permission.

The publisher acknowledges gratefully the following sources:
The English translation of the Roman *Lectionary for Mass*, copyright ©
1969, 1980, 1981; International Committee on English in the Liturgy,
Inc. All rights reserved.
The lectionary from the *Lutheran Book of Worship*, copyright © 1978 by
the Lutheran Church in America, The American Lutheran Church, the
Evangelical Lutheran Church of Canada, and the Lutheran Church-
Missouri Synod. All rights reserved.
The lectionary from the *Book of Common Prayer*, copyright © 1977 by
Charles Mortimer Guilbert as Custodian of the Standard Book of
Common Prayer. All rights reserved.

The Lectionary for the Christian People, Cycle B, copyright © 1987 Pueblo
Publishing Company, Inc. All rights reserved.
No part of this publication may be reproduced, stored
in a retrieval system, or transmitted in any form or by any means, electronic
mechanical, photocopying, recording, or otherwise, without the prior
permission of the publisher.

Library of Congress Cataloging-in-Publication Data

**Lectionary for the Christian people. Cycle B of the
Roman, Episcopal, Lutheran lectionaries.**

Intended for use in liturgy.
Emendations made to reduce the number of gender-
specific expressions.
Includes index.
1. Lectionaries—Texts.
BS391.2 1987   264'.34   87-45319
ISBN 0-916134-81-4 (Pueblo)
ISBN 0-8006-2081-X (Fortress Press)   *1-2081*

Printed in the United States of America

TABLE OF CONTENTS

Ordinary Time

Episcopal Lectionary

Lutheran Lectionary

INTRODUCTION

This volume continues the project begun with *Lectionary for the Christian People, Cycle A*, to offer the Sunday readings for the Roman, Episcopal, and Lutheran lectionaries. It includes Cycle B, as well as seven of the historic Paschal Vigil lessons and readings for several significant holy days.

The goal of this revision is to provide a translation of the lectionary based on the contemporary American English consensus concerning generic language. This lectionary is basically conservative in its maintenance of key biblical imagery, with the hope that it will be used extensively in average American parishes. Great attention has been given to the sound of the readings, since the lectionary is meant for public proclamation. The following are our general principles for revision:

1. The Revised Standard Version (RSV) has been chosen as the translation on which the revision is based because it is the most trustworthy and ecumenical biblical translation available for speakers of American English. It is an approved translation for Roman Catholics. Many revisions constitute a more faithful rendering of the Hebrew and Greek; others employ an altering of syntax required when translating one language into another. We invite those studying this lectionary to compare it with the original languages.

2. Masculine pronouns for God have been eliminated. At places participial constructions have been used, nouns appropriate to the context supplied. Occasionally, recalling the biblical tradition of describing divine action by using the circumlocution of passive voice, active verbs have been recast into the passive.

3. The dual rendering for LORD and Lord, as translations of the tetragrammaton and of *Kyrios*, has been retained as the best solution for the present. As well, this keeps the language of the lessons the same as the language of the liturgy.

4. Masculine pronouns for Jesus have been considerably reduced. The Christian conviction that God became incarnate in a particular male human being does allow us use of masculine

language for Christ. Following the classical christological understanding, no distinction has been made between Jesus of Nazareth and the risen Christ.

5. In Old Testament passages, which speak of the davidic messiah, which were understood as masculine, and which have been interpreted by Christians as signaling Christ, masculine references have been greatly reduced, but not wholly eliminated. The apocalyptic resonance of the New Testament title *huios tou anthropou*, usually translated "Son of Man," has been suggested by the translation "Man of Heaven."

6. Father and Son language has been retained for trinitarian titles. Jesus is the Son of the Father. When father appears in apposition to God, commas are inserted to distance the word God from the title Father. Jesus' calling of God Father in the gospels has been retained.

7. The *thou* used in the RSV in address to God has been changed to *you*.

8. Masculine designations as generic for humankind have been eliminated. Neither are occupational titles, such as shepherd, assumed to be masculine. Sometimes this results in casting the sentence in the plural, as is common now in American English. It is astounding how often masculine designations have entered the text in English translations and have no basis in the original language.

9. Many biblical passages are inconsistent in grammatical person, that is, alternating between second person plural (you) and third person singular (he). Rendering such passages with a more contemporary consistency, this lectionary uses either the second person plural (you) throughout or the third person plural (they) throughout, thus replacing the third person singular (he).

10. In narrative and parable no attempt has been made to generalize the sex of specific persons or to include persons of the opposite sex in a desire for balance. The original images of the story have been retained.

11. Greek narrative can refer to a specific named individual with a participial construction or within a verbal form in a way that English cannot. Contemporary usage suggests that at times "a man" or "a woman" be inserted.

12. Some lessons contain poetic formulations in which sexuality is ascribed to nongender-specific things or beings. In sustained conceits, as in the Lady Wisdom poems, the sexual imagery is retained. In isolated verses, as in reference to a city as *she* or to an angel as *he*, since contemporary English does not have grammatical gender, the sexual references are eliminated.

13. When translating the biblical source of common liturgical texts, as in the opening lines of the Gloria in excelsis in Luke 2, the attempt has been made to cast the translation in its most familiar contemporary liturgical form. Thus there are echoes of the ICET translations in this lectionary.

14. When a passage is extremely familiar, an attempt has been made to recast the syntax so that the revision does not sound like a mistake.

15. Because there is diversity among the churches in the way readings are begun, this lectionary has provided only such lead-in phrases (*incipits*) as are necessary for understanding. These lead-in phrases are drawn from the context and are in brackets. In certain gospel readings, we have added the traditional "at that time."

16. Proper names replace pronoun references in narratives to reduce "he" and to assist aural comprehension.

17. Some lessons, pp. 206 and 262, are essentially sexist in speaking specifically of a subordinate position of women. Such problematic lessons are translated faithful to the original, with the hope that future lectionary revisions will choose other readings as more appropriate for today's church. Such lessons are marked with a §.

18. The following are examples of recurring alterations:

king, in reference to God = Sovereign
king, in reference to Jesus or messiah = king usually retained

king, in reference to humankind = ruler, unless a named king
kingdom of God = dominion of God
kingdom on earth = realm or country or kingdom
God our Father = God, our Father
father, in Hebrew image for God = "as father"
fathers, as in ancestors = forebears
men of X, in direct address = O Xeans
sons, as generic term = children
God himself = that very God
by his mercy = out of mercy, God
Son of Man = Man of Heaven
he who = the one who, those who
brethren, in direct address = my dear people
brethren, in reference to group = the community or similar
    phrase
fellowship = communion
member, of human body = physical part
babe = infant
the paralytic = the one paralyzed
in travail = in labor pangs
the circumcized = the Jewish people
the Jews = depending on context: the Judeans, the Jewish peo-
    ple, the Jews
anthropos, anthropon = depending on context: mortals, human
    beings, person, humankind, a man, others, people, every-
    one, those

However, euphony or specific context may have led to a differ-
ent decision in revision.

Translation always requires choices between subtleties. In order
to gain inclusiveness we have pluralized texts ("he" becomes
"they") and have thereby sometimes diminished directness. Replacing "his people" with "the people of God" may seem to
create distance. A few words cannot say all the truth at once.

In this volume we continue the work begun in the volume of
Cycle A to provide the readings for a selection of ecumenically
shared holy days. The lessons for January 1, February 2, and

August 15 have not been reprinted in this volume, but are available in Cycle A.

Unfortunately, we have not been able to include revisions of the psalm for the day. Several inclusive language translations of the psalms are available: *Consultation on a Liturgical Psalter* (Washington, DC: International Commission on English in the Liturgy, 1984) and Gary Chamberlain's *The Psalms: A New Translation for Prayer and Worship* (Nashville: The Upper Room, 1984).

We hope that this lectionary will prove of service to the liturgical assemblies of our lands.

Gordon W. Lathrop
Gail Ramshaw

A GUIDE TO THE USE OF THE LECTIONARY

Find the Sunday or Feast Day according to the title used in:

R—the Roman Catholic lectionary and sacramentary
E—the American Episcopalian *Book of Common Prayer*
L—the *Lutheran Book of Worship*

Find the reading to be proclaimed. The chapter and verses indicated in the official liturgical books are listed and are also marked:

R—the Roman Catholic lectionary according to the *Editio Typica*,
    second edition
E—the lectionary of the *Book of Common Prayer*
L—the lectionary of the *Lutheran Book of Worship*

Note that when two or more official lectionaries agree on the reading, even partially, the full biblical passage involved is printed only once.

Identify the verses in the printed passage that are proper to your community's lectionary. Verse numbers are included in the printed passage only where necessary to identify beginnings, endings, and omitted passages. If verses are to be omitted, readers will have to be attentive to sentence structure, supplying missing words from the context. The difference between Latin syntax and the English of this translation suggests that sometimes more verses and fuller sentences should be proclaimed than are called for in the *Editio Typica*. Note that occasionally the Latin versification of the Roman lectionary differs from the numbering found in English language translations. That difference has been noted.

Supply the reading with the introductory words and concluding phrases proper to your community's use.

Note further:

• Seven readings for the Vigil of Easter have been included. They are printed in the longest and most inclusive form in which they appear in any of the lectionaries. They have not been marked according to denominational use, but together they provide a sufficient selection to meet the requirements of all three sets of liturgical books.

• The sign § is used to mark readings currently included in the official lectionaries in which the essential problems of inclusivity and sexism cannot be resolved by translation or responsible linguistic emendation.

FIRST READING

R Isaiah 63:16b–17, 19b; 64:2b–7
E Isaiah 64:1–9a
L Isaiah 63:16b–17; 64:1–8

[16b]You, O Lord, are father to us,
    our Redeemer from of old is your name.
[17]O Lord, why do you make us err from your ways
    and harden our heart, so that we fear you not?
Return for the sake of your servants,
    the tribes of your heritage.
[19b/1]O that you would rend the heavens and come down,
    that the mountains might quake at your presence—
[1a/2]as when fire kindles brushwood
    and the fire causes water to boil—
to make your name known to your adversaries,
    and that the nations might tremble at your presence!
[2b/3]When you did terrible things which we looked not for,
    you came down, the mountains quaked at your presence.
From of old no one has heard
    or perceived by the ear,
no eye has seen a God besides you,
    who works for those who await you.
You meet those who joyfully work righteousness,
    those who remember you in your ways.
Behold, you were angry, and we sinned;
    in our sins we have been a long time, and shall we be saved?
We have all become like one who is unclean,
    and all our righteous deeds are like a polluted garment.
We all fade like a leaf,
    and our iniquities, like the wind, take us away.
There is no one that calls upon your name,
    who arises to take hold of you;
for you have hid your face from us,
    and have delivered us into the hand of our iniquities.
[7/8]Yet, O Lord, you are father to us;
    we are the clay, and you are our potter;

we are all the work of your hand.
9aBe not exceedingly angry, O Lord,
    and remember not iniquity for ever.

SECOND READING

R L   1 Corinthians 1:3–9
E   1 Corinthians 1:1–9

1Paul, called by the will of God to be an apostle of Christ Jesus, and our brother Sosthenes,

To the church of God which is at Corinth, to those sanctified in Christ Jesus, called to be saints together with all those who in every place call on the name of our Lord Jesus Christ, both their Lord and ours:

3Grace to you and peace from God, our Father, and the Lord Jesus Christ.

I give thanks to God always for you because of the grace of God which was given you in Christ Jesus, that in every way you were enriched in Christ with all speech and all knowledge—even as the testimony to Christ was confirmed among you—so that you are not lacking in any spiritual gift, as you wait for the revealing of our Lord Jesus Christ; who will sustain you to the end, guiltless in the day of our Lord Jesus Christ. 9God is faithful, by whom you were called into the communion of the Son of God, Jesus Christ our Lord.

GOSPEL

R E L   Mark 13:33–37

[At that time Jesus said,]

33"Take heed, watch; for you do not know when the time will come. It is like someone going on a journey, who leaving home and putting the servants in charge of their work, commands the doorkeeper to be on the watch. Watch therefore—for you do not know when the lord of the house will come, in the evening, or at midnight, or at cockcrow, or in the morning—lest the lord come suddenly and find you asleep. 37And what I say to you I say to all: Watch."

FIRST READING

R Isaiah 40:1–5, 9–11
E L Isaiah 40:1–11

¹Comfort, comfort my people, says your God.
Speak tenderly to Jerusalem,
   and cry to the city
that its warfare is ended,
   that its iniquity is pardoned,
that it has received from the LORD's hand
   double for all its sins.
A voice cries:
"In the wilderness prepare the way of the LORD,
   make straight in the desert a highway for our God.
Every valley shall be lifted up,
   and every mountain and hill be made low;
the uneven ground shall become level,
   and the rough places a plain.
⁵And the glory of the LORD shall be revealed,
   and all flesh shall see it together,
   for the mouth of the LORD has spoken."
⁶A voice says, "Cry!"
   And I said, "What shall I cry?"
All flesh is grass,
   and all its beauty is like the flower of the field.
The grass withers, the flower fades,
   when the breadth of the LORD blows upon it;
   surely the people is grass.
The grass withers, the flower fades;
   but the word of our God will stand for ever.
⁹Get you up to a high mountain,
   O Zion, herald of good tidings;
lift up your voice with strength,
   O Jerusalem, herald of good tidings,
   lift it up, fear not;
say to the cities of Judah,

"Behold your God!"
Behold, the Lord GOD comes with might,
    with an arm to rule;
behold, God comes bearing the reward,
    preceded by the recompense.
[11]The LORD will feed the chosen flock like a shepherd;
    God's arms will gather the lambs.
God's bosom will bear them up;
    the LORD will gently lead those that are with young.

SECOND READING

R L   2 Peter 3:8–14
E   2 Peter 3:8–15a, 18

[8]Do not ignore this one fact, beloved, that with the Lord one day is as a thousand years, and a thousand years as one day. The Lord is not slow concerning the promise as some count slowness, but is forbearing toward you, not wishing that any should perish, but that all should reach repentance. But the day of the Lord will come like a thief, and then the heavens will pass away with a loud noise, and the elements will be dissolved with fire, and the earth and the works that are upon it will be burned up.

Since all these things are thus to be dissolved, what sort of persons ought you to be in lives of holiness and godliness, waiting for and hastening the coming of the day of the God, because of which the heavens will be kindled and dissolved, and the elements will melt with fire! But according to God's promise we wait for new heavens and a new earth in which righteousness dwells.

[14]Therefore, beloved, since you wait for these, be zealous to be found by God without spot or blemish, and at peace. [15a]And count the forbearance of our Lord as salvation. [18]But grow in the grace and knowledge of our Lord and Savior Jesus Christ, to whom be the glory both now and to the day of eternity. Amen.

GOSPEL

Mark 1:1–8

¹The beginning of the gospel of Jesus Christ, the Son of God.

As it is written in Isaiah the prophet,
    "Behold, I send my messenger before your face,
who shall prepare your way;
the voice of one crying in the wilderness:
Prepare the way of the Lord,
make straight the paths of the Lord—"

John the baptizer appeared in the wilderness, preaching a baptism of repentance for the forgiveness of sins. And there went out to him all the country of Judea, and all the people of Jerusalem; and they were baptized by him in the river Jordan, confessing their sins. Now John was clothed with camel's hair, and had a leather belt around his waist, and ate locusts and wild honey. And he preached, saying, "After me comes one who is mightier than I, the thong of whose sandals I am not worthy to stoop down and untie. ⁸I have baptized you with water; but the one who is coming will baptize you with the Holy Spirit."

FIRST READING

R Isaiah 61:1–2a, 10–11
L Isaiah 61:1–3, 10–11

¹The Spirit of the Lord GOD is upon me,
   because the LORD has anointed me
to bring good tidings to the afflicted;
   the LORD has sent me to bind up the brokenhearted,
to proclaim liberty to the captives,
   and the opening of the prison to those who are bound;
²ᵃto proclaim the year of the LORD's favor,
   and the day of vengeance of our God;
²ᵇto comfort all who mourn;
³to grant to those who mourn in Zion—
   to give them a garland instead of ashes,
the oil of gladness instead of mourning,
   the mantle of praise instead of a faint spirit;
that they may be called oaks of righteousness,
   the planting of the LORD, that God may be glorified.
¹⁰I will greatly rejoice in the LORD,
   my soul shall exult in my God;
for God has clothed me with the garments of salvation,
   and covered me with the robe of righteousness,
as a bridegroom decks himself with a garland,
   and as a bride adorns herself with her jewels.
¹¹For as the earth brings forth its shoots,
   and as a garden causes what is sown in it to spring up,
so the Lord GOD will cause righteousness and praise
   to spring forth before all the nations.

E Isaiah 65:17–25

¹⁷"For behold, I create new heavens
   and a new earth;
and the former things shall not be remembered
   or come into mind.
But be glad and rejoice for ever

in that which I create;
for behold, I create Jerusalem a rejoicing,
　　and its people a joy.
I will rejoice in Jerusalem,
　　and be glad in my people;
no more shall be heard in it the sound of weeping
　　and the cry of distress.
No more shall there be in it
　　an infant that lives but a few days,
　　or aged folk who do not fill out their days,
for the child shall die a hundred years old,
　　and those who fall short of a hundred years shall be reviled.
They shall build houses and inhabit them;
　　they shall plant vineyards and eat their fruit.
They shall not build and another inhabit;
　　they shall not plant and another eat;
for like the days of a tree shall the days of my people be,
　　and my chosen shall long enjoy the work of their hands.
They shall not labor in vain,
　　or bear children for calamity;
for they shall be the offspring of the blessed of the LORD,
　　and their children with them.
Before they call I will answer,
　　while they are yet speaking I will hear.
25The wolf and the lamb shall feed together,
　　the lion shall eat straw like the ox;
　　and dust shall be the serpent's food.
They shall not hurt or destroy
　　in all my holy mountain, says the LORD."

SECOND READING

R L　1 Thessalonians 5:16–24
　E　1 Thessalonians 5:16–28

16Rejoice always, pray constantly, give thanks in all circumstances; for this is the will of God in Christ Jesus for you. Do not quench the Spirit, do not despise prophesying, but test everything; hold fast what is good, abstain from every form of evil.

May that very God of peace sanctify you wholly; and may your spirit and soul and body be kept sound and blameless at the coming of our Lord Jesus Christ. [24]God who calls you is faithful and will do it.

[25]My dear people, pray for us.

Greet the whole community with a holy kiss.

I adjure you by the Lord that this letter be read to the whole community.

[28]The grace of our Lord Jesus Christ be with you.

GOSPEL

R E L   John 1:6–8, 19–28

[6]There was sent by God a person named John. He came for testimony, to bear witness to the light, that all might believe through him. [8]He was not the light, but came to bear witness to the light.

[19]And this is the testimony of John, when the Jewish people sent priests and Levites from Jerusalem to ask him, "Who are you?" John confessed and did not deny, but confessed, "I am not the Christ." And they asked him, "What then? Are you Elijah?" John said, "I am not." "Are you the prophet?" And he answered, "No." They said to him then, "Who are you? Let us have an answer for those who sent us. What do you say about yourself?" John said, "I am the voice of one crying in the wilderness, 'Make straight the way of the Lord,' as the prophet Isaiah said."

Now they had been sent from the Pharisees. They asked him, "Then why are you baptizing, if you are neither the Christ, nor Elijah, nor the prophet?" John answered them, "I baptize with water; but among you stands one whom you do not know, even the one who comes after me, the thong of whose sandal I am not worthy to untie." [28]This took place in Bethany beyond the Jordan, where John was baptizing.

FIRST READING

R 2 Samuel 7:1–5, 8b–12, 14a, 16
E 2 Samuel 7:4, 8–16
L 2 Samuel 7:1–11, 16

[1]Now when King David dwelt in his house, and the LORD had given him rest from all his enemies round about, the king said to Nathan the prophet, "See now, I dwell in a house of cedar, but the ark of God dwells in a tent." And Nathan said to the king, "Go, do all that is in your heart; for the LORD is with you."

[4]But that same night the word of the LORD came to Nathan, [5]"Go and tell my servant David, 'Thus says the LORD: Would you build me a house to dwell in? [6]I have not dwelt in a house since the day I brought up the people of Israel from Egypt to this day, but I have been moving about in a tent for my dwelling. In all places where I have moved with all the people of Israel, did I speak a word with any of the judges of Israel, whom I commanded to shepherd my people Israel, saying, "Why have you not built me a house of cedar?" ' [8a]Now therefore thus you shall say to my servant David, [8b]'Thus says the LORD of hosts, I took you from the pasture, from following the sheep, that you should be prince over my people Israel; and I have been with you wherever you went, and have cut off all your enemies from before you; and I will make for you a great name, like the name of the great ones of the earth. And I will appoint a place for my people Israel, and will plant them, that they may dwell in their own place, and be disturbed no more; and the children of violence shall afflict them no more, as formerly, [11]from the time that I appointed judges over my people Israel; and I will give you rest from all your enemies. Moreover the LORD declares to you that the LORD will make you a house. [12]When your days are fulfilled and you lie down with your forebears, I will raise up your child after you, who shall come forth from your body, and I will establish his kingdom. [13]He shall build a house for my name, and I will establish the throne

of his dominion for ever. ¹⁴ᵃI will be as father to him, and he shall be as my son. ¹⁴ᵇWhen he commits iniquity, I will chasten him with the rod of a man, with the blows which human beings give; but I will not take my steadfast love from him, as I took it from Saul, whom I put away from before you. ¹⁶And your house and your dominion shall be made sure for ever before me; your throne shall be established for ever.' "

SECOND READING

R E L   Romans 16:25–27

²⁵Now to the one who is able to strengthen you according to my gospel and the preaching of Jesus Christ, according to the revelation of the mystery which was kept secret for long ages but is now disclosed and through the prophetic writings is made known to all nations, according to the command of the eternal God, to bring about the obedience of faith—²⁷to the only wise God be glory for evermore through Jesus Christ! Amen.

GOSPEL

R E L   Luke 1: 26–38

²⁶In the sixth month the angel Gabriel was sent from God to a city of Galilee named Nazareth, to a virgin betrothed to a man whose name was Joseph, of the house of David; and the virgin's name was Mary. And the angel came to her and said, "Hail, O favored one, the Lord is with you!" But she was greatly troubled at the saying, and considered in her mind what sort of greeting this might be. And the angel said to her, "Do not be afraid, Mary, for you have found favor with God. And behold, you will conceive in your womb and bear a son, and you shall call his name Jesus.

"He will be great, and will be called the Son of the Most High; and the Lord God will give to him the throne of his ancestor David,
and he will reign over the house of Jacob for ever;
and of his dominion there will be no end."

And Mary said to the angel, "How shall this be, since I am a virgin?" And the angel said to her,

"The Holy Spirit will come upon you,
and the power of the Most High will overshadow you;
therefore the child to be born will be called holy,
the Son of God.

"And behold, your kinswoman Elizabeth in her old age has also conceived a son; and this is the sixth month with her who was called barren. For with God nothing will be impossible." [38] And Mary said, "Behold, I am the serving maid of the Lord; let it be to me according to your word." And the angel departed from her.

R CHRISTMAS MASS AT MIDNIGHT
E CHRISTMAS DAY I
L THE NATIVITY OF OUR LORD, 1

FIRST READING

R L   Isaiah 9:2–7
   E   Isaiah 9:2–4, 6–7

²The people who walked in darkness
   have seen a great light;
those who dwelt in a land of deep darkness,
   on them has light shined.
You have multiplied the nation,
   you have increased its joy;
they rejoice before you
   as with joy at the harvest,
   as they rejoice when dividing spoil.
⁴For the yoke of their burden,
   and the staff of their shoulders,
   the rod of their oppressor,
   you have broken as on the day of Midian.
⁵For every boot of the tramping warrior in battle tumult
   and every garment rolled in blood
   will be burned as fuel for the fire.
⁶For to us a child is born,
   to us a son is given;
and the government will be upon his shoulder,
   and his name will be called
"Wonderful Counselor, Mighty God,
   Everlasting Father, Prince of Peace."
⁷Of the greatness of his government and of peace
   there will be no end,
upon the throne and dominion of David,
   to establish it, and to uphold it
with justice and with righteousness
   from this time forth and for evermore.
The zeal of the LORD of hosts will do this.

12 CHRISTMAS MASS AT MIDNIGHT   R
    CHRISTMAS DAY I   E
    THE NATIVITY OF OUR LORD, 1   L

SECOND READING

R E L   Titus 2:11–14

¹¹The grace of God has appeared for the salvation of all people, training us to renounce irreligion and worldly passions, and to live sober, upright, and godly lives in this world, awaiting our blessed hope, the appearing of the glory of the great God and our Savior Jesus Christ, ¹⁴who gave himself for us to redeem us from all iniquity and to purify for himself a chosen people who are zealous for good deeds.

GOSPEL

R E   Luke 2:1–14
L   Luke 2:1–20

¹In those days a decree went out from Caesar Augustus that all the world should be enrolled. This was the first enrollment, when Quirinius was governor of Syria. And all went to their own city to be enrolled. And Joseph also went up from Galilee, from the city of Nazareth, to Judea, to the city of David, which is called Bethlehem, because he was of the house and lineage of David, to be enrolled with Mary, his betrothed, who was with child. And while they were there, the time came for her to deliver. And she gave birth to her first-born son and wrapped him in swaddling cloths, and laid him in a manger, because there was no place for them in the inn.

And in that region there were shepherds out in the field, keeping watch over their flock by night. And an angel of the Lord appeared to them, and the glory of the Lord shone around them, and they were filled with fear. And the angel said to them, "Be not afraid; for behold, I bring you good news of a great joy which will come to all the people; for to you is born this day in the city of David a Savior, who is Christ the Lord. And this will be a sign for you: you will find an infant wrapped in swaddling cloths and lying in a manger." And suddenly there was with the angel a multitude of the heavenly host praising God and saying,

¹⁴"Glory to God in the highest,
and peace to God's people on earth."

R   CHRISTMAS MASS AT MIDNIGHT   13
E   CHRISTMAS DAY I
L   THE NATIVITY OF OUR LORD, 1

[15]And when the angels went away from them into heaven, the shepherds said to one another, "Let us go over to Bethlehem and see this thing that has happened, which the Lord has made known to us." And they went with haste, and found Mary and Joseph, and the infant lying in a manger. And when they saw it they made known the saying which had been told them concerning this child; and all who heard it wondered at what the shepherds told them. But Mary kept all these things, pondering them in her heart. [20]And the shepherds returned, glorifying and praising God for all they had heard and seen, as it had been told them.

FIRST READING

R   Isaiah 62:11–12
E   Isaiah 62:6–7, 10–12
L   Isaiah 62:10–12

⁶Upon your walls, O Jerusalem,
   I have placed sentries;
all the day and all the night
   they shall never be silent.
You who put the LORD in remembrance,
   take no rest,
⁷and give to God no rest
   until Jerusalem is established
   and made a praise in the earth.
¹⁰Go through, go through the gates,
   prepare the way for the people;
build up, build up the highway,
   clear it of stones,
   lift up an ensign over the peoples.
¹¹Behold, the LORD has proclaimed
   to the end of the earth:
Say to daughter Zion,
   "Behold, your salvation comes;
behold, God comes bearing the reward,
   preceded by the recompense."
¹²And they shall be called The holy people,
   The redeemed of the LORD;
and you shall be called Sought out,
   a city not forsaken.

SECOND READING

R E L   Titus 3:4–7

⁴When the goodness and loving kindness of God our Savior appeared, we were saved, not because of deeds done by us in righteousness, but in virtue of God's own mercy, by the washing of regeneration and renewal in the Holy Spirit, poured out upon us richly through Jesus Christ our Savior, ⁷so that we might be justified by God's grace and become heirs in hope of eternal life.

GOSPEL

R E   Luke 2:15–20
L   Luke 2:1–20

¹In those days a decree went out from Caesar Augustus that all the world should be enrolled. This was the first enrollment, when Quirinius was governor of Syria. And all went to their own city to be enrolled. And Joseph also went up from Galilee, from the city of Nazareth, to Judea, to the city of David, which is called Bethlehem, because he was of the house and lineage of David, to be enrolled with Mary, his betrothed, who was with child. And while they were there, the time came for her to deliver. And she gave birth to her first-born son and wrapped him in swaddling cloths, and laid him in a manger, because there was no place for them in the inn.

And in that region there were shepherds out in the field, keeping watch over their flock by night. And an angel of the Lord appeared to them, and the glory of the Lord shone around them, and they were filled with fear. And the angel said to them, "Be not afraid; for behold, I bring you good news of a great joy which will come to all the people; for to you is born this day in the city of David a Savior, who is Christ the Lord. And this will be a sign for you: you will find an infant wrapped in swaddling cloths and lying in a manger." And suddenly there was with the angel a multitude of the heavenly host praising God and saying,

"Glory to God in the highest,
and peace to God's people on earth."

[15]And when the angels went away from them into heaven, the shepherds said to one another, "Let us go over to Bethlehem and see this thing that has happened, which the Lord has made known to us." And they went with haste, and found Mary and Joseph, and the infant lying in a manger. And when they saw it they made known the saying which had been told them concerning this child; and all who heard it wondered at what the shepherds told them. But Mary kept all these things, pondering them in her heart. [20]And the shepherds returned, glorifying and praising God for all they had heard and seen, as it had been told them.

R CHRISTMAS MASS DURING THE DAY
E CHRISTMAS DAY III
L THE NATIVITY OF OUR LORD, 2

FIRST READING

R E L   Isaiah 52:7–10

⁷How beautiful upon the mountains
    are the feet of the messenger,
who publishes peace, who brings good tidings of good,
    who publishes salvation,
    who says to Zion, "Your God reigns."
Hark, your sentries lift up their voice,
    together they sing for joy;
for with their own eyes they see
    the return of the LORD to Zion.
Break forth together into singing,
    you waste places of Jerusalem;
for the LORD has comforted the people
    and has redeemed Jerusalem.
¹⁰The holy arm of the LORD is bared
    before the eyes of all the nations,
and all the ends of the earth shall see
    the salvation of our God.

SECOND READING

R   Hebrews 1:1–6
E   Hebrews 1:1–12
L   Hebrews 1:1–9

¹In many and various ways God spoke of old to our forebears
by the prophets; but in these last days God has spoken to us by
the Son, whom God appointed the heir of all things, and
through whom God also created the world. This Son reflects
the glory of God and bears the very stamp of God's nature,
upholding the universe by a word of power. The Son, having
made purification for sins, sat down at the right hand of the
Majesty on high, having become as much superior to angels as
the name the Son has obtained is more excellent than theirs.

For to what angel did God ever say,

"You are my Son,
today I have begotten you"?

Or again,

"I will be to him as father,
and he shall be to me as son"?

⁶And again, bringing the first-born into the world, God says,

"Let all God's angels worship him."

⁷Of the angels God says,

"God makes the angels winds,
God's servants flames of fire."

But of the Son God says,

"Your throne, O God, is for ever and ever,
the righteous scepter is the scepter of your dominion.
⁹You have loved righteousness and hated lawlessness;
therefore God, your God, has anointed you
with the oil of gladness beyond your comrades."

¹⁰And,

"You, Lord, founded the earth in the beginning,
and the heavens are the work of your hands;
they will perish, but you remain;
they will all grow old like a garment,
¹²like a mantle you will roll them up,
and they will be changed.
But you are the same,
and your years will never end."

GOSPEL

R   John 1:1–18
E L   John 1:1–14

¹In the beginning was the Word, and the Word was with God,
and the Word was God. The Word was in the beginning with
God; all things were made through the Word, without whom

nothing that was made was made. In the Word was life, and the life was the light of all. The light shines in the darkness, and the darkness has not overcome it.

There was sent by God a person named John. He came for testimony, to bear witness to the light, that all might believe through him. He was not the light, but came to bear witness to the light.

The true light that enlightens everyone was coming into the world. The light was in the world, and the world was made through the light, yet the world knew him not. He came to his own home, and his own people received him not. But to all who received him, who believed in his name, he gave power to become children of God; who were born, not of blood nor of the will of the flesh nor of the desire of a man, but of God.

[14]And the Word became flesh and dwelt among us, full of grace and truth; we have beheld his glory, glory as of the only Son from the Father. [15](John bore witness to the Word, and cried, "This is the one of whom I said, 'The one who comes after me ranks before me, for he was before me.' ") And from the Son's fullness have we all received, grace upon grace. For the law was given through Moses; grace and truth came through Jesus Christ. [18]No one has ever seen God; the only Son, who is in the bosom of the Father, has made God known.

R HOLY FAMILY

E L FIRST SUNDAY AFTER CHRISTMAS

FIRST READING

R Genesis 15:1–6; 21:1–3

¹The word of the LORD came to Abram in a vision, "Fear not, Abram, I am your shield; your reward shall be very great." But Abram said, "O Lord GOD, what will you give me, for I continue childless, and the heir of my house is Eliezer of Damascus?" And Abram said, "Behold, you have given me no offspring; and a slave born in my house will be my heir." And behold, the word of the LORD came to him, "This man shall not be your heir; your own offspring shall be your heir." And the LORD brought Abram outside and said, "Look toward heaven, and number the stars, if you are able to number them." Then the LORD said to him, "So shall your descendants be." ⁶And Abram believed the LORD; and the LORD reckoned it to him as righteousness.

¹The LORD visited Sarah as had been said, and the LORD did to Sarah as had been promised. And Sarah conceived, and bore Abraham a son in his old age at the time of which God had spoken to him. ³Abraham called the name of his son who was born to him, whom Sarah bore him, Isaac.

E Isaiah 61:10–62:3

¹⁰I will greatly rejoice in the LORD,
   my soul shall exult in my God;
for God has clothed me with the garments of salvation,
   and covered me with the robe of righteousness,
as a bridegroom decks himself with a garland,
   and as a bride adorns herself with her jewels.
For as the earth brings forth its shoots,
   and as a garden causes what is sown in it to spring up,
so the Lord GOD will cause righteousness and praise
   to spring forth before all the nations.
For Zion's sake I will not keep silent,
   and for Jerusalem's sake I will not rest,

until its vindication goes forth as brightness
   and its salvation as a burning torch.
The nations shall see your vindication,
   and all the rulers your glory;
and you shall be called by a new name
   which the mouth of the LORD will give.
³You shall be a crown of beauty in the hand of the LORD,
   and a royal diadem in the hand of your God.

L   Isaiah 45:22–25

[Thus says the LORD:]

   ²²"Turn to me and be saved,
   all the ends of the earth!
   For I am God, and there is no other.
By myself I have sworn,
   from my mouth has gone forth in righteousness
   a word that shall not return;
'To me every knee shall bow,
   every tongue shall swear.'
Only in the LORD, it shall be said of me,
   are righteousness and strength;
to the LORD shall come and be ashamed,
   all who were incensed against God.
²⁵In the LORD all the offspring of Israel
   shall triumph and glory."

SECOND READING

R   Hebrews 11:8, 11–12, 17–19

⁸By faith Abraham obeyed when he was called to go out to a
place which he was to receive as an inheritance; and he went
out, not knowing where he was to go. ¹¹By faith Sarah herself
received power to conceive, even when she was past the age,
since she considered faithful the one who had promised.
¹²Therefore from one man, and him as good as dead, were
born descendants as many as the stars of heaven and as the
innumerable grains of sand by the seashore.

¹⁷By faith Abraham, when he was tested, offered up Isaac, and he who had received the promises was ready to offer up his only son, of whom it was said, "Through Isaac shall your descendants be named." ¹⁹He considered that God was able even to raise the dead; hence, figuratively speaking, Abraham did receive Isaac back.

E   Galatians 3:23–25; 4:4–7

²³Now before faith came, we were confined under the law, kept under restraint until faith should be revealed. So that the law was our custodian until Christ came, that we might be justified by faith. ²⁵But now that faith has come, we are no longer under a custodian.

⁴When the time had fully come, God sent forth the Son, born of woman, born under the law, to redeem those who were under the law, so that we might receive adoption. And because you are adopted children, God has sent the Spirit of the Son into our hearts, crying, "Abba! Father!" ⁷So through God you are no longer a slave but an adopted child, and if a child then an heir.

L   Colossians 3:12–17

¹²Put on then, as God's chosen ones, holy and beloved, compassion, kindness, lowliness, meekness, and patience, forbearing one another and, if one has a complaint against another, forgiving each another; as the Lord has forgiven you, so you also must forgive. And above all these put on love, which binds everything together in perfect harmony. And let the peace of Christ rule in your hearts, to which indeed you were called in the one body. And be thankful. Let the word of Christ dwell in you richly, teach and admonish one another in all wisdom, and sing psalms and hymns and spiritual songs with thankfulness in your hearts to God. ¹⁷And whatever you do, in word or deed, do everything in the name of the Lord Jesus, giving thanks to God, the Father, through him.

GOSPEL

R Luke 2:22–40
L Luke 2:25–40

²²When the time came for their purification according to the law of Moses, Mary and Joseph brought Jesus up to Jerusalem to present him to the Lord (as it is written in the law of the Lord, "Every male that opens the womb shall be called holy to the Lord") and to offer a sacrifice according to what is said in the law of the Lord, "a pair of turtledoves, or two young pigeons." ²⁵Now there was in Jerusalem a person named Simeon, who was righteous and devout, looking for the consolation of Israel, and the Holy Spirit was upon him. And it had been revealed to him by the Holy Spirit that he should not see death before he had seen the Lord's Christ. And inspired by the Spirit Simeon came into the temple; and when the parents brought in the child Jesus, to do for him according to the custom of the law, he took Jesus up in his arms, and blessed God and said,

"Lord, now you let your servant go in peace;
your word has been fulfilled.
My own eyes have seen the salvation
which you have prepared in the sight of every people:
a light to reveal you to the nations
and the glory of your people Israel."

And his father and his mother marveled at what was said about Jesus; and Simeon blessed them and said to Mary his mother,

"Behold, this child is set for the fall and rising of many in
    Israel,
and for a sign that is spoken against
(and a sword will pierce through your own soul also),
that thoughts out of many hearts may be revealed."

And there was a prophetess, Anna, the daughter of Phanuel, of the tribe of Asher; she was of a great age, having lived with her husband seven years from her marriage, and as a widow till she was eighty-four. She did not depart from the temple, worshiping with fasting and prayer night and day. And coming up at that very hour she gave thanks to God, and spoke of the child to all who were looking for the redemption of Jerusalem.

And when the parents had performed everything according to the law of the Lord, they returned into Galilee, to their own city, Nazareth. ⁴⁰And the child grew and became strong, filled with wisdom; and the favor of God was upon him.

E   John 1:1–18

¹In the beginning was the Word, and the Word was with God, and the Word was God. The Word was in the beginning with God; all things were made through the Word, without whom nothing that was made was made. In the Word was life, and the life was the light of all. The light shines in the darkness, and the darkness has not overcome it.

There was sent by God a person named John. He came for testimony, to bear witness to the light, that all might believe through him. He was not the light, but came to bear witness to the light.

The true light that enlightens everyone was coming into the world. The light was in the world, and the world was made through the light yet the world knew him not. He came to his own home, and his own people received him not. But to all who received him, who believed in his name, he gave power to become children of God; who were born, not of blood nor of the will of the flesh nor of the desire of a man, but of God.

And the Word became flesh and dwelt among us, full of grace and truth; we have beheld his glory, glory as of the only Son from the Father. (John bore witness to the Word, and cried, "This is the one of whom I said, 'The one who comes after me ranks before me, for he was before me.' ") And from the Son's fullness have we all received, grace upon grace. For the law was given through Moses; grace and truth came through Jesus Christ. ¹⁸No one has ever seen God; the only Son, who is in the bosom of the Father, has made God known.

FIRST READING

R Sirach 24:1–2, 8–12

¹Wisdom will praise herself,
  and will glory in the midst of her people.
²In the assembly of the Most High she will open her mouth,
  and in the presence of God's host she will glory:
⁸"The Creator of all things gave me a commandment,
  and the one who created me assigned a place for my tent,
Saying, 'Make your dwelling in Jacob,
  and in Israel receive your inheritance.'
From eternity, in the beginning, the Most High created me,
  and for eternity I shall not cease to exist.
In the holy tabernacle I ministered before the Most High,
  and so I was established in Zion.
In the beloved city likewise I received a resting place,
  and in Jerusalem was my dominion.
¹²So I took root in an honored people,
  in the portion of the Lord, who is their inheritance."

E Jeremiah 31:7–14

⁷For thus says the LORD:
"Sing aloud with gladness for Jacob,
  and raise shouts for the chief of the nations;
proclaim, give praise, and say,
  'The LORD has saved the remnant of Israel, the people of the
    LORD.'
Behold, I will bring them from the north country,
  and gather them from the farthest parts of the earth,
among them those who are blind and lame,
  the woman with child and her who is in labor, together;
  a great company, they shall return here.
With weeping they shall come,
  and with consolations I will lead them back,
I will make them walk by brooks of water,
  in a straight path in which they shall not stumble;

for I am as a father to Israel,
    and Ephraim is as my first-born.
Hear the word of the LORD, O nations,
    and declare it in the coastlands afar off;
say, 'The one who scattered Israel's people will gather them
    and will keep them as a shepherd keeps the flock.'
For the LORD has ransomed Jacob,
    and has redeemed Jacob from hands too strong for them.
They shall come and sing aloud on the height of Zion,
    and they shall be radiant over the goodness of the LORD,
over the grain, the wine, and the oil,
    and over the young of the flock and the herd;
their life shall be like a watered garden,
    and they shall languish no more.
Then shall the maidens rejoice in the dance,
    and the young men and the old shall be merry.
I will turn their mourning into joy,
    I will comfort them, and give them gladness for sorrow.
¹⁴I will feast the soul of the priests with abundance,
    and my people shall be satisfied with my goodness,
        says the LORD."

L   Isaiah 61:10–62:3

¹⁰I will greatly rejoice in the LORD,
    my soul shall exult in my God;
for God has clothed me with the garments of salvation,
    and covered me with the robe of righteousness,
as a bridegroom decks himself with a garland,
    and as a bride adorns herself with her jewels.
For as the earth brings forth its shoots,
    and as a garden causes what is sown in it to spring up,
so the Lord GOD will cause righteousness and praise
    to spring forth before all the nations.
For Zion's sake I will not keep silent,
    and for Jerusalem's sake I will not rest,
until its vindication goes forth as brightness
    and its salvation as a burning torch.
The nations shall see your vindication,

and all the rulers your glory;
and you shall be called by a new name
which the mouth of the LORD will give.
³You shall be a crown of beauty in the hand of the LORD,
and a royal diadem in the hand of your God.

SECOND READING

R L Ephesians 1:3–6, 15–18
E   Ephesians 1:3–6, 15–19a

³Blessed be the God and Father of our Lord Jesus Christ, who
has blessed us in Christ with every spiritual blessing in the
heavenly places, even as God chose us in Christ before the
foundation of the world, that before God we should be holy
and blameless. God destined us in love for adoption through
Jesus Christ: this was God's good pleasure and will, ⁶to the
praise of God's glorious grace freely bestowed on us in the
Beloved.

¹⁵For this reason, because I have heard of your faith in the
Lord Jesus and your love toward all the saints, I do not cease to
give thanks for you, remembering you in my prayers, that the
God of our Lord Jesus Christ, the Father of glory, may give you
a spirit of wisdom and of revelation, that you may know God,
¹⁸having the eyes of your hearts enlightened, that you may
know what is the hope to which God has called you, what are
the riches of God's glorious inheritance in the saints, ¹⁹ᵃand
what is the immeasurable greatness of God's power in us who
believe.

GOSPEL

R L John 1:1–18

¹In the beginning was the Word, and the Word was with God,
and the Word was God. The Word was in the beginning with
God; all things were made through the Word, without whom
nothing that was made was made. In the Word was life, and
the life was the light of all. The light shines in the darkness,
and the darkness has not overcome it.

There was sent by God a person named John. He came for testimony, to bear witness to the light, that all might believe through him. He was not the light, but came to bear witness to the light.

The true light that enlightens everyone was coming into the world. The light was in the world, and the world was made through the light, yet the world knew him not. He came to his own home, and his own people received him not. But to all who received him, who believed in his name, he gave power to become children of God; who were born, not of blood nor of the will of the flesh nor of the desire of a man, but of God.

And the Word became flesh and dwelt among us, full of grace and truth; we have beheld his glory, glory as of the only Son from the Father. (John bore witness to the Word, and cried, "This is the one of whom I said, 'The one who comes after me ranks before me, for he was before me.' ") And from the Son's fullness have we all received, grace upon grace. For the law was given through Moses; grace and truth came through Jesus Christ. [18]No one has ever seen God: the only Son, who is in the bosom of the Father, has made God known.

E   Matthew 2:13–15, 19–23

[13]Now when the magi had departed, behold, an angel of the Lord appeared to Joseph in a dream and said, "Rise, take the child and his mother, and flee to Egypt, and remain there till I tell you; for Herod is about to search for the child, to destroy him." And Joseph rose and took the child and his mother by night, and departed to Egypt, [15]and remained there until the death of Herod. This was to fulfill what the Lord had spoken by the prophet, "Out of Egypt have I called my son."

[19]But when Herod died, behold, an angel of the Lord appeared in a dream to Joseph in Egypt, saying, "Rise, take the child and his mother, and go to the land of Israel, for those who sought the child's life are dead." And Joseph rose and took the child and his mother, and went to the land of Israel. But when he

heard that Archelaus reigned over Judea in place of his father Herod, he was afraid to go there, and being warned in a dream he withdrew to the district of Galilee. [23]And he went and dwelt in a city called Nazareth, that what was spoken by the prophets might be fulfilled, "He shall be called a Nazarene."

FIRST READING

R L Isaiah 60:1–6
E Isaiah 60:1–6, 9

¹Arise, shine; for your light has come,
  and the glory of the LORD has risen upon you.
For behold, darkness shall cover the earth,
  and thick darkness the peoples;
but the LORD will arise upon you,
  and the glory of the LORD will be seen upon you.
And nations shall come to your light,
  and rulers to the brightness of your rising.
Lift up your eyes round about, and see;
  they all gather together, they come to you;
your sons shall come from far,
  and your daughters shall be carried in the arms.
Then you shall see and be radiant,
  your heart shall thrill and rejoice;
because the abundance of the sea shall be turned to you,
  the wealth of the nations shall come to you.
⁶A multitude of camels shall cover you,
  the young camels of Midian and Ephah;
  all those from Sheba shall come.
They shall bring gold and frankincense,
  and shall proclaim the praise of the LORD.
⁹For the coastlands shall wait for me,
  the ships of Tarshish first,
to bring your children from far,
  their silver and gold with them,
for the name of the LORD your God,
  and for the Holy One of Israel,
  because your God has glorified you.

SECOND READING

R   Ephesians 3:2–3a, 5–6
E   Ephesians 3:1–12
L   Ephesians 3:2–12

¹For this reason I, Paul, a prisoner for Christ Jesus on behalf of you Gentiles—²assuming that you have heard of the stewardship of God's grace that was given to me for you, ³ᵃhow the mystery was made known to me by revelation, ³ᵇas I have written briefly. When you read this you can perceive my insight into the mystery of Christ, ⁵which was not made known to people of other generations as it has now been revealed to his holy apostles and prophets by the Spirit; ⁶that is, how the Gentiles are heirs with us, members of the same body, and partakers of the promise in Christ Jesus through the gospel.

⁷Of this gospel I was made a minister according to the gift of God's grace which was given me by the working of God's power. To me, though I am the very least of all the saints, this grace was given, to preach to the Gentiles the unsearchable riches of Christ, and to make everyone see what is the plan of the mystery hidden for ages in God who created all things; that through the church the manifold wisdom of God might now be made known to the principalities and powers in the heavenly places. This was according to the eternal purpose which God has realized in Christ Jesus our Lord, ¹²through faith in whom we have boldness and confidence of access to God.

GOSPEL

R E L   Matthew 2:1–12

¹Now when Jesus was born in Bethlehem of Judea in the days of Herod the king, behold, magi from the East came to Jerusalem, saying, "Where is he who has been born king of the Jews? For we have seen his star in the East, and have come to worship him." When Herod the king heard this, he was troubled, and all Jerusalem with him; and assembling all the chief priests and scribes of the people, he inquired of them where the Christ

was to be born. They told him, "In Bethlehem of Judea; for so it is written by the prophet:

'And you, O Bethlehem, in the land of Judah,
are by no means least among the rulers of Judah;
for from you shall come a ruler
who will govern my people Israel.' "

Then Herod summoned the magi secretly and ascertained from them what time the star appeared; and he sent them to Bethlehem, saying, "Go and search diligently for the child, and when you have found him bring me word, that I too may come and worship." When they had heard the king they went their way; and lo, the star which they had seen in the East went before them, till it came to rest over the place where the child was. When they saw the star, they rejoiced exceedingly with great joy; and going into the house they saw the child with Mary his mother, and they fell down and worshiped him. Then, opening their treasures, they offered him gifts, gold and frankincense and myrrh. [12]And being warned in a dream not to return to Herod, they departed to their own country by another way.

R L BAPTISM OF OUR LORD
E FIRST SUNDAY AFTER THE EPIPHANY

FIRST READING

R Isaiah 42:1–4, 6–7
E Isaiah 42:1–9
L Isaiah 42:1–7

¹Behold my servant, whom I uphold,
   my chosen, in whom my soul delights,
upon whom I have put my Spirit,
   to bring forth justice to the nations:
not crying out, not lifting up his voice,
   not making it heard in the street,
a bruised reed my servant will not break,
   nor quench a dimly burning wick,
   but will faithfully bring forth justice.
⁴My chosen one will not fail or be discouraged
   till he has established justice in the earth;
   and the coastlands wait for his law.
⁵Thus says God, the LORD,
   who created the heavens and stretched them out,
   who spread forth the earth and what comes from it,
who gives breath to the people upon it
   and spirit to those who walk in it:
⁶"I am the LORD, I have called you in righteousness,
   I have taken you by the hand and kept you;
I have given you as a covenant to the people,
   a light to the nations,
   ⁷to open the eyes that are blind,
to bring out the prisoners from the dungeon,
   from the prison those who sit in darkness.
⁸I am the LORD, that is my name;
   my glory I give to no other,
   nor my praise to graven images.
⁹Behold, the former things have come to pass,
   and new things I now declare;

before they spring forth
  I tell you of them."

SECOND READING

R E L Acts 10:34–38

[34]Peter opened his mouth and said: "Truly I perceive that God shows no partiality, but in every nation any one who is God-fearing and does what is right is acceptable to God. You know the word which God sent to Israel, preaching good news of peace by Jesus Christ (who is Lord of all), the word which was proclaimed throughout all Judea, beginning from Galilee after the baptism which John preached: [38]how God anointed Jesus of Nazareth with the Holy Spirit and with power; how Jesus went about doing good and healing all that were oppressed by the devil, for God was with him."

GOSPEL

R E Mark1:7–11
 L Mark 1:4–11

[4]John the baptizer appeared in the wilderness, preaching a baptism of repentance for the forgiveness of sins. And there went out to him all the country of Judea, and all the people of Jerusalem; and they were baptized by him in the river Jordan, confessing their sins. Now John was clothed with camel's hair, and had a leather belt around his waist, and ate locusts and wild honey. [7]And John preached, saying, "After me comes one who is mightier than I, the thong of whose sandals I am not worthy to stoop down and untie. I have baptized you with water; but the one who is coming will baptize you with the Holy Spirit."

In those days Jesus came from Nazareth of Galilee and was baptized by John in the Jordan. And coming up out of the water, immediately Jesus saw the heavens opened and the Spirit descending upon him like a dove; [11]and a voice came from heaven, "You are my son, the beloved one; with you I am well pleased."

R SECOND SUNDAY IN ORDINARY TIME
E L SECOND SUNDAY AFTER THE EPIPHANY

FIRST READING

R   1 Samuel 3:3b–10, 19
E L 1 Samuel 3:1–10

¹The young Samuel was ministering to the Lord under Eli.
And the word of the Lord was rare in those days; there was no
frequent vision.

At that time Eli, whose eyesight had begun to grow dim, so
that he could not see, was lying down in his own place; the
lamp of God had not yet gone out, and ³ᵇSamuel was lying
down within the temple of the Lord, where the ark of God
was. Then the Lord called, "Samuel! Samuel!" and he said,
"Here I am!" and ran to Eli, and said, "Here I am, for you
called me." But Eli said, "I did not call; lie down again." So
Samuel went and lay down. And the Lord called again, "Samuel!" And Samuel arose and went to Eli, and said, "Here I am,
for you called me." But Eli said, "I did not call, my son; lie
down again." Now Samuel did not yet know the Lord, and the
word of the Lord had not yet been revealed to him. And the
Lord called Samuel again the third time. And he arose and
went to Eli, and said, "Here I am, for you called me." Then Eli
perceived that the Lord was calling the boy. Therefore Eli said
to Samuel, "Go, lie down; and if the Lord calls you, you shall
say, 'Speak, Lord, for your servant hears.' " So Samuel went
and lay down in his place.

¹⁰And the Lord came and stood forth, calling as at other times,
"Samuel! Samuel!" And Samuel said, "Speak, for your servant
hears."

¹⁹And Samuel grew, and the Lord was with him and let none
of his words fall to the ground.

SECOND READING

R 1 Corinthians 6:13c–15a, 17–20
E 1 Corinthians 6:11b–20
L 1 Corinthians 6:12–20

[11b]You were washed, you were sanctified, you were justified in the name of the Lord Jesus Christ and in the Spirit of our God.

[12]"All things are lawful for me," but not all things are helpful. "All things are lawful for me," but I will not be enslaved by anything. "Food is meant for the stomach and the stomach for food"—and God will destroy both one and the other. [13c]The body is not meant for immorality, but for the Lord, and the Lord for the body. And God raised the Lord and will also raise us up by divine power. [15a]Do you not know that your bodies are physical parts of Christ? [15b]Shall I therefore take the parts of Christ and make them parts of a prostitute? Never! Do you not know that the one who unites with a prostitute becomes one body with that prostitute? For, as it is written, "The two shall become one flesh." [17]But the one who is united to the Lord becomes one spirit with the Lord. Shun immoral sexual conduct. Every other sin which is committed is outside the body; but immoral sexual conduct is sin against one's own body. Do you not know that your body is a temple of the Holy Spirit within you, which you have from God? You are not your own; [20]you were bought with a price. So glorify God in your body.

GOSPEL

R John 1:35–42

[35]John was standing with two of his disciples; and he looked at Jesus walking by, and said, "Behold, the Lamb of God!" The two disciples heard him say this, and they followed Jesus. Jesus turned, and saw them following, and said to them, "What do you seek?" And they said to him, "Rabbi" (which means Teacher), "where are you staying?" Jesus said to them, "Come and see." They came and saw where he was staying; and they stayed with him that day, for it was about the tenth hour. One

of the two who heard John speak, and followed him, was Andrew, Simon Peter's brother. He first found his brother Simon, and said to him, "We have found the Messiah" (which means Christ). [42]Andrew brought Simon to Jesus. Jesus looked at him, and said, "So you are Simon the son of John? You shall be called Cephas" (which means Peter).

E L   John 1:43–51

[43]Jesus decided to go to Galilee. And he found Philip and said to him, "Follow me." Now Philip was from Bethsaida, the city of Andrew and Peter. Philip found Nathanael, and said to him, "We have found the one of whom Moses in the law and also the prophets wrote, Jesus of Nazareth, the son of Joseph." Nathanael said to Philip, "Can anything good come out of Nazareth?" Philip said to him, "Come and see." Jesus saw Nathanael coming to him, and said of him, "Behold, an Israelite indeed, in whom is no guile!" Nathanael said to Jesus, "How do you know me?" Jesus answered him, "Before Philip called you, when you were under the fig tree, I saw you." Nathanael answered him, "Rabbi, you are the Son of God! You are the King of Israel!" Jesus answered him, "Because I said to you, I saw you under the fig tree, do you believe? You shall see greater things than these." [51]And Jesus said to him, "Truly, truly, I say to you, you will see heaven opened, and the angels of God ascending and descending upon the Man of Heaven."

R THIRD SUNDAY IN ORDINARY TIME
E L THIRD SUNDAY AFTER THE EPIPHANY

FIRST READING

R L Jonah 3:1–5, 10

¹The word of the LORD came to Jonah the second time, saying, "Arise, go to Nineveh, that great city, and proclaim to it the message that I tell you." So Jonah arose and went to Nineveh, according to the word of the LORD. Now Nineveh was an exceedingly great city, three days' journey in breadth. Jonah began to go into the city, going a day's journey. And he cried, "Yet forty days, and Nineveh shall be overthrown!" ⁵And the people of Nineveh believed God; they proclaimed a fast, and put on sackcloth, from the greatest of them to the least of them.

¹⁰When God saw what they did, how they turned from their evil way, God repented of the evil which had been threatened; and God did not do it.

E Jeremiah 3:21–4:2

²¹A voice on the bare heights is heard,
　the weeping and pleading of the children of Israel,
because they have perverted their way,
　they have forgotten the LORD their God.
"Return, O faithless people,
　I will heal your faithlessness."
"Behold, we come to you;
　for you are the LORD our God.
Truly the hills are a delusion,
　the orgies on the mountains.
Truly in the LORD our God
　is the salvation of Israel.

"But from our youth the shameful thing has devoured all for which our forebears labored, their flocks and their herds, their sons and their daughters. Let us lie down in our shame, and let our dishonor cover us; for we have sinned against the LORD our

God, we and our forebears, from our youth even to this day;
and we have not obeyed the voice of the LORD our God."

"If you return, O Israel, says the LORD,
   to me you should return.
If you remove your abominations from my presence,
   and do not waver,
²and if you swear, 'As the LORD lives,'
   in truth, in justice, and in uprightness,
then nations shall bless themselves in you,
   and in you shall they glory."

SECOND READING

R L   I Corinthians 7:29–31

²⁹My dear people, the appointed time has grown very short;
from now on, let those who are married live as though they
were not, and those who mourn as though they were not
mourning, and those who rejoice as though they were not rejoicing, and those who buy as though they had no goods,
³¹and those who deal with the world as though they had no
dealings with it. For the form of this world is passing away.

E   1 Corinthians 7:17–23

¹⁷Let each one of you lead the life which the Lord has assigned
to you, and in which God has called you. This is my rule in all
the churches. Was any one of you at the time of the call already
circumcised? Do not seek to remove the marks of circumcision.
Was any one of you at the time of the call uncircumcised? Do
not seek circumcision. For neither circumcision counts for anything nor uncircumcision, but keeping the commandments of
God. Every one of you should remain in the state in which you
were called. Were you a slave when called? Never mind. But if
you can gain your freedom, avail yourself of the opportunity.
For whoever was called in the Lord as a slave is free before the
Lord. Likewise whoever was free when called is enslaved to
Christ. ²³You were bought with a price; do not become slaves
of others.

GOSPEL

Mark 1:14–20

[14]After John was arrested, Jesus came into Galilee, preaching the gospel of God, and saying, "The time is fulfilled, and the dominion of God is at hand; repent, and believe in the gospel."

And passing along by the Sea of Galilee, Jesus saw Simon and Andrew the brother of Simon casting a net in the sea; for they were fishermen. And Jesus said to them, "Follow me and I will make you fish for human beings." And immediately they left their nets and followed him. And going on a little farther, Jesus saw James the son of Zebedee and John his brother, who were in their boat mending the nets. [20]And immediately Jesus called them; and they left their father Zebedee in the boat with the hired servants, and followed him.

R FOURTH SUNDAY IN ORDINARY TIME
E L FOURTH SUNDAY AFTER THE EPIPHANY

FIRST READING

R E L Deuteronomy 18:15–20

[Moses said to the people,]

¹⁵"The Lᴏʀᴅ your God will raise up for you a prophet like me from among you, from your kinfolk—whom you shall heed—just as you desired of the Lᴏʀᴅ your God at Horeb on the day of the assembly, when you said, 'Let me not hear again the voice of the Lᴏʀᴅ my God, or see this great fire any more, lest I die.' And the Lᴏʀᴅ said to me, 'They have rightly said all that they have spoken. I will raise up for them a prophet like you from among their kin; and I will put my words in his mouth, to speak all that I command. And those who do not give heed to my words which the prophet shall speak in my name, I myself will require it of them. ²⁰But the prophet who presumes to speak a word in my name which I have not commanded him to speak, or who speaks in the name of other gods, that same prophet shall die.' "

SECOND READING

R 1 Corinthians 7:32–35

³²I want you to be free from anxieties. The unmarried man is anxious about the affairs of the Lord, how to please the Lord; but the married man is anxious about wordly affairs, how to please his wife, and his interests are divided. And the unmarried woman or virgin is anxious about the affairs of the Lord, how to be holy in body and spirit; but the married woman is anxious about worldly affairs, how to please her husband. ³⁵I say this for your own benefit, not to lay any restraint upon you, but to promote good order and to secure your undivided devotion to the Lord.

E   1 Corinthians 8:1b–13
L   1 Corinthians 8:1–13

[1]Now concerning food offered to idols: we know that "all of us possess knowledge." [1b]"Knowledge" puffs up, but love builds up. Those who imagine that they know something do not yet know as they ought to know. But if one loves God, one is known by God.

Hence, as to the eating of food offered to idols, we know that "an idol has no real existence," and that "there is no God but one." For although there may be so-called gods in heaven or on earth—as indeed there are many "gods" and many "lords"—yet for us there is one God, the Father, from whom are all things and for whom we exist, and one Lord, Jesus Christ, through whom are all things and through whom we exist.

However, not all possess this knowledge. But some, through being hitherto accustomed to idols, eat food as really offered to an idol; and their conscience, being weak, is defiled. Food will not commend us to God. We are no worse off if we do not eat, and no better off if we do. Only take care lest this liberty of yours somehow become a stumbling block to the weak. For if any one sees you, a person of knowledge, at table in an idol's temple, might that one, having a weak conscience, not be encouraged to eat food offered to idols? And so by your knowledge this weak person, this dear one for whom Christ died, is destroyed. Thus, sinning against those in your community and wounding their conscience when it is weak, you sin against Christ. [13]Therefore, if food causes my brother or sister to fall, I will never eat meat, lest I cause offense in the community.

GOSPEL

R E L   Mark 1:21–28

[21]Jesus and his followers went into Capernaum; and immediately on the sabbath he entered the synagogue and taught. And they were astonished at his teaching, for Jesus taught them as one who had authority, and not as the scribes. And immediately there was in their synagogue a man with an unclean spirit, who cried out, "What have you to do with us, Jesus of

Nazareth? Have you come to destroy us? I know who you are, the Holy One of God." But Jesus rebuked the spirit, saying, "Be silent, and come out of him!" And the unclean spirit, convulsing him and crying with a loud voice, came out of the man. And they were all amazed, so that they questioned among themselves, saying, "What is this? A new teaching! With authority he commands even the unclean spirits, and they obey him." [28]And at once Jesus' fame spread everywhere throughout all the surrounding region of Galilee.

FIRST READING

R Job 7:1–4, 6–7
L Job 7:1–7

[Job answered,]

¹Has not a man a hard service upon earth,
  and are not his days like the days of a hireling?
Like a slave who longs for the shadow,
  and like a hireling who looks for wages,
so I am allotted months of emptiness,
  and nights of misery are apportioned to me.
⁴When I lie down I say, 'When shall I arise?'
  But the night is long,
  and I am full of tossing till the dawn.
⁵My flesh is clothed with worms and dirt;
  my skin hardens, then breaks out afresh.
⁶My days are swifter than a weaver's shuttle,
  and come to their end without hope.
⁷Remember that my life is a breath;
  my eye will never again see good.

E 2 Kings 4:18–21, 32–37

¹⁸When the child of the Shunammite had grown, he went out
one day to his father among the reapers. And he said to his
father, "Oh, my head, my head!" The father said to his servant,
"Carry him to his mother." And when the servant had lifted
him, and brought him to his mother, the child sat on her lap till
noon, and then he died. ²¹And she went up and laid him on
the bed of Elisha, the man of God, and shut the door upon
him, and went out.

³²When Elisha came into the house, he saw the child lying
dead on his bed. So he went in and shut the door upon the
two of them, and prayed to the LORD. Then he went up and
lay upon the child, putting his mouth upon the child's mouth,

his eyes upon his eyes, and his hands upon his hands; and as Elisha stretched himself upon the child, the flesh of the child became warm. Then Elisha got up again, and walked once to and fro in the house, and went up, and stretched himself upon the child; the child sneezed seven times, and opened his eyes. Then Elisha summoned Gehazi and said, "Call this Shunammite." So Gehazi called her. And when she came to Elisha, he said, "Take up your son." [37]She came and fell at his feet, bowing to the ground; then she took up her son and went out.

SECOND READING

R 1 Corinthians 9:16–19, 22–23
E L 1 Corinthians 9:16–23

[16]If I preach the gospel, that gives me no ground for boasting. For necessity is laid upon me. Woe to me if I do not preach the gospel! For if I do this of my own will, I have a reward; but if not of my own will, I am entrusted with a commission. What then is my reward? Just this: that in my preaching I may make the gospel free of charge, not making full use of my right in the gospel.

[19]For though I am free from all people, I have made myself a slave to all, that I might win the more. [20]To the Jews I became as a Jew, in order to win Jews; to those under the law I became as one under the law—though not being myself under the law—that I might win those under the law. To those outside the law I became as one outside the law—not being without law toward God but under the law of Christ—that I might win those outside the law. [22]To the weak I became weak, that I might win the weak. I have become all things to all people, that I might by all means save some. [23]I do it all for the sake of the gospel, that I may share in its blessings.

GOSPEL

R E L Mark 1:29–39

²⁹Immediately Jesus left the synagogue, and entered the house of Simon and Andrew, with James and John. Now Simon's mother-in-law lay sick with a fever, and immediately they told Jesus of her. And Jesus came and took her by the hand and lifted her up, and the fever left her; and she served them.

That evening, at sundown, they brought to Jesus all who were sick or possessed with demons. And the whole city was gathered together about the door. And Jesus healed many who were sick with various diseases, and cast out many demons; and he would not permit the demons to speak, because they knew him.

And in the morning, a great while before day, Jesus rose and went out to a lonely place, and there he prayed. And Simon and those who were with him pursued him, and they found Jesus and said to him, "Every one is searching for you." And Jesus said to them, "Let us go on to the next towns, that I may preach there also; for that is why I came out." ³⁹And Jesus went throughout all Galilee, preaching in their synagogues and casting out demons.

R SIXTH SUNDAY IN ORDINARY TIME
E L SIXTH SUNDAY AFTER THE EPIPHANY
E PROPER 1

FIRST READING

R Leviticus 13:1–2, 44–46

¹The LORD said to Moses and Aaron, ²"When the skin of some-one's body has a swelling or an eruption or a spot, and it turns into a leprous disease on the body's skin, then that person shall be brought to Aaron the priest or to one of his descendants the priests.

⁴⁴"If he is a leprous man, he is unclean; the priest must pro-nounce him unclean; his disease is on his head. The male leper who has the disease shall wear torn clothes and let the hair of his head hang loose, and he shall cover his upper lip and cry, 'Unclean, unclean.' ⁴⁶He shall remain unclean as long as he has the disease; he is unclean; he shall dwell alone in a habitation outside the camp."

E 2 Kings 5:1–15ab
L 2 Kings 5:1–14

¹Naaman, commander of the army of the king of Syria, was a great man with his master and in high favor, because by him the LORD has given victory to Syria. He was a mighty man of valor, but he was a leper. Now the Syrians on one of their raids had carried off a young girl from the land of Israel, and she waited on Naaman's wife. She said to her mistress, "Would that my master were with the prophet who is in Samaria! He would cure him of his leprosy." So Naaman went in and told his master, "Thus and so spoke the girl from the land of Is-rael." And the king of Syria said, "Go now, and I will send a letter to the king of Israel."

So Naaman went, taking with him ten talents of silver, six thou-sand shekels of gold, and ten festal garments. And he brought the letter to the king of Israel, which read, "When this letter reaches you, know that I have sent to you Naaman my servant, that you may cure him of his leprosy." And when the king of

Israel read the letter, he rent his clothes and said, "Am I God, to kill and to make alive, that this man sends word to me to cure a man of his leprosy? Only consider, and see how he is seeking a quarrel with me."

But when Elisha the man of God heard that the king of Israel had rent his clothes, he sent to the king, saying, "Why have you rent your clothes? Let him come now to me, that he may know that there is a prophet in Israel." So Naaman came with his horses and chariots, and halted at the door of Elisha's house. And Elisha sent a messenger to him, saying, "Go and wash in the Jordan seven times, and your flesh shall be restored, and you shall be clean." But Naaman was angry, and went away, saying, "Behold, I thought that he would surely come out to me, and stand, and call on the name of the LORD his God, and wave his hand over the place, and cure the leper. Are not Abana and Pharpar, the rivers of Damascus, better than all the waters of Israel? Could I not wash in them, and be clean?" So he turned and went away in a rage. But his servants came near and said to him, "Dear master, if the prophet had commanded you to do some great thing, would you not have done it? How much rather, then, when he says to you, 'Wash, and be clean'?" ¹⁴So Naaman went down and dipped himself seven times in the Jordan, according to the word of the man of God; and his flesh was restored like the flesh of a little child, and he was clean.

¹⁵Then Naaman returned to the man of God, he and all his company, and he came and stood before Elisha; and he said, "Behold, I know that there is no God in all the earth but in Israel."

SECOND READING

R   1 Corinthians 10:31–11:1

³¹Whether you eat or drink, or whatever you do, do all to the glory of God. Give no offense to Jews or to Greeks or to the church of God, just as I try to please every one in everything I do, not seeking my own advantage, but that of many, that they may be saved. ¹Be imitators of me, as I am of Christ.

E L   1 Corinthians 9:24–27

²⁴Do you not know that in a race all the runners compete, but only one receives the prize? So run that you may obtain it. Every athlete exercises self-control in all things. They do it to receive a perishable wreath, but we an imperishable. Well, I do not run aimlessly, I do not box as one beating the air; ²⁷but I pummel my body and subdue it, lest after preaching to others I myself should be disqualified.

GOSPEL

R E L   Mark 1:40–45

⁴⁰A leprous man came, beseeching Jesus, and kneeling said to him, "If you will, you can make me clean." Moved with pity, Jesus stretched out his hand and touched him, and said to him, "I will; be clean." And immediately the leprosy left the man, and he was made clean. And Jesus sternly charged the man, and sent him away at once, saying, "See that you say nothing to any one; but go, show yourself to the priest, and offer for your cleansing what Moses commanded, for a proof to the people." ⁴⁵But the one who was cleansed went out and began to talk freely about it, and to spread the news, so that Jesus could no longer openly enter a town, but was out in the country; and people came to him from every quarter.

FIRST READING

R   Isaiah 43:18–19, 21–22, 24b–25
E L Isaiah 43:18–25

[Thus says the LORD:]

¹⁸"Remember not the former things,
  nor consider the things of old.
¹⁹Behold, I am doing a new thing;
  now it springs forth, do you not perceive it?
I will make a way in the wilderness
  and rivers in the desert.
²⁰The wild beasts will honor me,
  the jackals and the ostriches;
for I give water in the wilderness,
  rivers in the desert,
to give drink to my chosen people,
  ²¹the people whom I formed for myself
that they might declare my praise.
²²Yet you did not call upon me, O Jacob;
  but you have been weary of me, O Israel!
²³You have not brought me your sheep for burnt offerings,
  or honored me with your sacrifices.
I have not burdened you with offerings,
  or wearied you with frankincense.
You have not bought me sweet cane with money,
  or satisfied me with the fat of your sacrifices.
²⁴ᵇBut you have burdened me with your sins,
  you have wearied me with your iniquities.
²⁵I, I am the one
  who blots out your transgressions for my own sake,
  and I will not remember your sins."

SECOND READING

R E L   2 Corinthians 1:18–22

[18]As surely as God is faithful, our word to you has not been Yes and No. For the Son of God, Jesus Christ, whom we, Silvanus and Timothy and I, preached among you, was not Yes and No; but in Christ it is always Yes. For all the promises of God find their Yes in him. That is why we utter the Amen through Christ, to the glory of God. But it is God who establishes us with you in Christ, and has commissioned us. [22]It is God who has also sealed us and has given us the Spirit in our hearts as a guarantee.

GOSPEL

R E L   Mark 2:1–12

[1]When Jesus returned to Capernaum after some days, it was reported that he was at home. And many were gathered together, so that there was no longer room for them, not even about the door; and he was preaching the word to them. And they came, bringing to Jesus a paralyzed man carried by four people. And when they could not get near Jesus because of the crowd, they removed the roof above him; and when they had made an opening, they let down the pallet on which the paralyzed man lay. And when Jesus saw their faith, he said to the paralyzed man, "My child, yours sins are forgiven." Now some of the scribes were sitting there, questioning in their hearts, "Why does this man speak thus? It is blasphemy! Who can forgive sins but God alone?" And immediately Jesus, perceiving in his spirit that they thus questioned within themselves, said to them, "Why do you question thus in your hearts? Which is easier, to say to the paralyzed man, 'Your sins are forgiven,' or to say, 'Rise, take up your pallet and walk'? But that you may know that the Man of Heaven has authority on earth to forgive sins"—he said to the paralyzed man—"I say to you, rise, take up your pallet and go home." [12]And the man rose, and immediately took up the pallet and went out before them all; so that they were all amazed and glorified God, saying, "We never saw anything like this!"

FIRST READING

R Hosea 2:16b, 17b, 21–22

E Hosea 2:14–23

L Hosea 2:14–16, 19–20

[Thus says the LORD:]

$^{16a/14}$"Behold, I will allure you,
^{16b}and I will bring you into the wilderness,
   and speak tenderly to you.
^{17a}And there I will give you your vineyards,
   and make the Valley of Achor a door of hope.
^{17b}And there you shall answer as in the days of your youth,
   as at the time when you came out of the land of Egypt.

$^{18/16}$"And in that day, says the LORD, you will call me 'My husband,' and no longer will you call me, 'My master.' ^{17}For I will remove the names of the master Baals from your mouth, and they shall be mentioned by name no more. And I will make for you a covenant on that day with the beasts of the field, the birds of the air, and the creeping things of the ground; and I will abolish the bow, the sword, and war from the land; and I will make you lie down in safety. $^{21/19}$And I will betroth you to me for ever; I will betroth you to me in righteousness and in justice, in steadfast love, and in mercy. $^{22/20}$I will betroth you to me in faithfulness; and you shall know the LORD.

^{21}"And in that day, says the LORD,
   I will answer the heavens
   and they shall answer the earth;
and the earth shall answer the grain, the wine, and the oil,
   and they shall answer God-sows;
^{23}and I will sow you for myself in the land.
And I will have pity on Not-pitied,
   and I will say to Not-my-people, 'You are my people';
   and you shall say, 'You are my God.' "

SECOND READING

R L   2 Corinthians 3:1b–6

¹ᵇDo we need, as some do, letters of recommendation to you, or from you? You yourselves are our letter of recommendation, written on your hearts, to be known and read by all; and you show that you are a letter from Christ delivered by us, written not with ink but with the Spirit of the living God, not on tablets of stone but on tablets of human hearts.

Such is the confidence that we have through Christ toward God. Not that we are competent of ourselves to claim anything as coming from us; our competence is from God, ⁶who has made us competent to be ministers of a new covenant, not in a written code but in the Spirit; for the written code kills, but the Spirit gives life.

E   2 Corinthians 3:17–4:2

¹⁷The Lord is the Spirit, and where the Spirit of the Lord is, there is freedom. And we all, with unveiled face, beholding the glory of the Lord, are being changed from one degree of glory to another into the likeness of the Lord; for this comes from the Lord who is the Spirit.

Therefore, having this ministry by the mercy of God, we do not lose heart. ²We have renounced disgraceful, underhanded ways; we refuse to practice cunning or to tamper with God's word, but by the open statement of the truth we would commend ourselves to every one's conscience in the sight of God.

GOSPEL

R E L   Mark 2:18–22

¹⁸John's disciples and the Pharisees were fasting; and people came and said to Jesus, "Why do John's disciples and the disciples of the Pharisees fast, but your disciples do not fast?" And Jesus said to them, "Can the wedding guests fast while the bridegroom is with them? As long as they have the bridegroom with them, they cannot fast. The days will come, when the bridegroom is taken away from them, and then they will fast in that day. No one sews a piece of unshrunk cloth on an old

garment; for the patch would tear away from it, the new from the old, and a worse tear would be made. [22]And no one puts new wine into old wineskins; for the wine would burst the skins, and the wine would be lost, and the skins as well; but new wine is for fresh skins."

E LAST SUNDAY AFTER THE EPIPHANY
L TRANSFIGURATION OF OUR LORD

FIRST READING

E 1 Kings 19:9–18

⁹Elijah came to a cave, and lodged there; and behold, the word of the LORD came to him, and said to him, "What are you doing here, Elijah?" Elijah said, "I have been very jealous for the LORD, the God of hosts; for the people of Israel have forsaken your covenant, thrown down your altars, and slain your prophets with the sword; and I, even I only, am left; and they seek my life, to take it away." And the LORD said, "Go forth, and stand upon the mount before the LORD." And behold, the LORD passed by, and a great and strong wind rent the mountains, and broke in pieces the rocks before the LORD, but the LORD was not in the wind; and after the wind an earthquake, but the LORD was not in the earthquake; and after the earthquake a fire, but the LORD was not in the fire; and after the fire a still small voice. And when Elijah heard it, he wrapped his face in his mantle and went out and stood at the entrance of the cave. And behold, there came a voice to him, and said, "What are you doing here, Elijah?" He said, "I have been very jealous for the LORD, the God of hosts; for the people of Israel have forsaken your covenant, thrown down your altars, and slain your prophets with the sword; and I, even I only, am left; and they seek my life, to take it away." And the LORD said to him, "Go, return on your way to the wilderness of Damascus; and when you arrive, you shall anoint Hazael to be king over Syria; and Jehu the son of Nimshi you shall anoint to be king over Israel; and Elisha the son of Shaphat of Abelmeholah you shall anoint to be prophet in your place. And the one who escapes from the sword of Hazael shall Jehu slay; and the one who escapes from the sword of Jehu shall Elisha slay. ¹⁸Yet I will leave seven thousand in Israel, all the knees that have not bowed to Baal, and every mouth that has not kissed him."

¹When the LORD was about to take Elijah up to heaven by a whirlwind, Elijah and Elisha were on their way from Gilgal. And Elijah said to Elisha, "Tarry here, I pray you; for the LORD has sent me as far as Bethel." But Elisha said, "As the LORD lives, and as you yourself live, I will not leave you." So they went down to Bethel. And the prophets who were in Bethel came out to Elisha, and said to him, "Do you know that today the LORD will take away your master from over you?" And Elisha said, "Yes, I know it; hold your peace."

Elijah said to him, "Elisha, tarry here, I pray you; for the LORD has sent me to Jericho." But Elisha said, "As the LORD lives, and as you yourself live, I will not leave you." So they came to Jericho. The prophets who were at Jericho drew near to Elisha, and said to him, "Do you know that today the LORD will take away your master from over you?" And he answered, "Yes, I know it; hold your peace."

Then Elijah said to Elisha, "Tarry here, I pray you; for the LORD has sent me to the Jordan." But Elisha said, "As the LORD lives, and as you yourself live, I will not leave you." So the two of them went on. Fifty men from among the prophets also went, and stood at some distance from them, as they both were standing by the Jordan. Then Elijah took his mantle, and rolled it up, and struck the water, and the water was parted to the one side and to the other, till the two of them could go over on dry ground.

When they had crossed, Elijah said to Elisha, "Ask what I shall do for you, before I am taken from you." And Elisha said, "I pray you, let me inherit a double share of your spirit." And Elijah said, "You have asked a hard thing; yet, if you see me as I am being taken from you, it shall be so for you; but if you do not see me, it shall not be so." And as they still went on and talked, behold, a chariot of fire and horses of fire separated the two of them. And Elijah went up by a whirlwind into heaven. ¹²ᵃAnd Elisha saw it and cried, "My father, my father! the chariot of Israel and its riders!" And Elisha saw Elijah no more.

SECOND READING

E   2 Peter 1:16–19

¹⁶For we did not follow cleverly devised myths when we made
known to you the power and coming of our Lord Jesus Christ,
but we were eyewitnesses of his majesty. For when Jesus our
Lord received honor and glory from God, the Father, and the
voice was borne to him by the Majestic Glory, "This is my Son,
my beloved one, with whom I am well pleased," we heard this
voice borne from heaven, for we were with Jesus on the holy
mountain. ¹⁹And we have the prophetic word made more sure.
You will do well to pay attention to this as to a lamp shining in
a dark place, until the day dawns and the morning star rises in
your hearts.

L   2 Corinthians 3:12–4:2

¹²Since we have such a hope, we are very bold, not like Moses,
who put a veil over his face so that the Israelites might not see
the end of the fading splendor. But their minds were hardened;
for to this day, when they read the old covenant, that same veil
remains unlifted, because only through Christ is it taken away.
Yes, to this day whenever Moses is read a veil lies over their
minds; but when one turns to the Lord the veil is removed.
Now the Lord is the Spirit, and where the Spirit of the Lord is,
there is freedom. And we all, with unveiled face, beholding the
glory of the Lord, are being changed from one degree of glory
to another into the likeness of the Lord; for this comes from the
Lord who is the Spirit.

Therefore, having this ministry by the mercy of God, we do not
lose heart. ²We have renounced disgraceful, underhanded
ways; we refuse to practice cunning or to tamper with God's
word, but by the open statement of the truth we would commend ourselves to every one's conscience in the sight of God.

GOSPEL

²After six days Jesus took with him Peter and James and John, and led them up a high mountain apart by themselves; and he was transfigured before them, and his garments became glistening, intensely white, as no fuller on earth could bleach them. And there appeared to them Elijah with Moses; and they were talking to Jesus. And Peter said to Jesus, "Rabbi, it is well that we are here; let us make three booths, one for you and one for Moses and one for Elijah." For he did not know what to say, for they were exceedingly afraid. And a cloud overshadowed them, and a voice came out of the cloud, "This is my Son, the beloved one; listen to him." And suddenly looking around they no longer saw any one with them but Jesus only.

⁹And as they were coming down the mountain, Jesus charged them to tell no one what they had seen, until the Man of Heaven should have risen from the dead.

FIRST READING

R   Joel 2:12–18
E   Joel 2:1–2, 12–17
L   Joel 2:12–19

¹Blow the trumpet in Zion;
   sound the alarm on my holy mountain!
Let all the inhabitants of the land tremble,
   for the day of the LORD is coming, it is near,
²a day of darkness and gloom,
   a day of clouds and thick darkness!
Like blackness there is spread upon the mountains
   a great and powerful people;
their like has never been from of old,
   nor will be again after them
   through the years of all generations.
¹²"Yet even now," says the LORD,
   "return to me with all your heart,
with fasting, with weeping, and with mourning;
   and rend your hearts and not your garments."
Return to the LORD, your God,
   for the LORD is gracious and merciful,
slow to anger, and abounding in steadfast love,
   and repents of evil.
Who knows whether the LORD will not turn and repent,
   and leave behind a blessing,
a cereal offering and a drink offering
   for the LORD, your God?
Blow the trumpet in Zion;
   sanctify a fast;
call a solemn assembly;
   gather the people.
Sanctify the congregation;
   assemble the elders;
gather the children,
   even nursing infants.

Let the bridegroom leave his room,
and the bride her chamber.
[17]Between the vestibule and the altar
let the priests, the ministers of the LORD, weep
and say, "Spare your people, O LORD,
and make not your heritage a reproach,
a byword among the nations.
Why should they say among the peoples,
'Where is their God?' "
[18]Then the LORD became jealous for the holy land,
and had pity on the people of God.
[19]The LORD answered and said to this people,
"Behold, I am sending to you
grain, wine, and oil,
and you will be satisfied;
and I will no more make you
a reproach among the nations."

SECOND READING

R 2 Corinthians 5:20–6:2
E 2 Corinthians 5:20b–6:10
L 2 Corinthians 5:20b–6:2

[20a]We are ambassadors for Christ, God appealing through us.
[20b]We beseech you on behalf of Christ, be reconciled to God.
For our sake God made the one who knew no sin to be sin, so
that in Christ we might become the righteousness of God.

Working together with God, then, we entreat you not to accept
God's grace in vain. [2]For God says,

"At the acceptable time I have listened to you,
and helped you on the day of salvation."

Behold, now is the acceptable time; behold, now is the day of
salvation. [3]We put no obstacle in any one's way, so that no
fault may be found with our ministry, but as servants of God
we commend ourselves in every way: through great endurance,
in afflictions, hardships, calamities, beatings, imprisonments, tu-
mults, labors, watching, hunger; by purity, knowledge, forbear-

ance, kindness, the Holy Spirit, genuine love, truthful speech, and the power of God; with the weapons of righteousness for the right hand and for the left; in honor and dishonor, in ill repute and good repute. We are treated as impostors, and yet are true; as unknown, and yet well known; as dying, and behold we live; as punished, and yet not killed; [10]as sorrowful, yet always rejoicing; as poor, yet making many rich; as having nothing, and yet possessing everything.

GOSPEL

R Matthew 6:1–6, 16–18
E L Matthew 6:1–6, 16–21

[At that time Jesus said,]

[1]"Beware of practicing your piety before others in order to be seen by them; for then you will have no reward from your Father who is in heaven.

"Thus, when you give alms, sound no trumpet before you, as the hypocrites do in the synagogues and in the streets, that they may be praised by others. Truly, I say to you, they have received their reward. But when you give alms, do not let your left hand know what your right hand is doing, so that your alms may be in secret; and your Father who sees in secret will reward you.

"And when you pray, you must not be like the hypocrites; for they love to stand and pray in the synagogues and at the street corners, that they may be seen by others. Truly, I say to you, they have received their reward. [6]But when you pray, go into your room and shut the door and pray to your Father who is in secret; and your Father who sees in secret will reward you.

[16]"And when you fast, do not look dismal, like the hypocrites, for they disfigure their faces that their fasting may be seen by others. Truly, I say to you, they have received their reward. But when you fast, anoint your head and wash your face, [18]that your fasting may not be seen by others but by your Father who is in secret; and your Father who sees in secret will reward you.

[19]"Do not lay up for yourselves treasures on earth, where moth and rust consume and where thieves break in and steal, but lay up for yourselves treasures in heaven, where neither moth nor rust consumes and where thieves do not break in and steal. [21]For where your treasure is, there will your heart be also."

FIRST READING

R Genesis 9:8–15
E Genesis 9:8–17

[8]God said to Noah and to Noah's sons with him, "Behold, I establish my covenant with you and your descendants after you, and with every living creature that is with you, the birds, the cattle, and every beast of the earth with you, as many as came out of the ark. I establish my covenant with you, that never again shall all flesh be cut off by the waters of a flood, and never again shall there be a flood to destroy the earth." And God said, "This is the sign of the covenant which I make between me and you and every living creature that is with you, for all future generations: I set my bow in the cloud, and it shall be a sign of the covenant between me and the earth. When I bring clouds over the earth and the bow is seen in the clouds, [15]I will remember my covenant which is between me and you and every living creature of all flesh; and the waters shall never again become a flood to destroy all flesh. [16]When the bow is in the clouds, I will look upon it and remember the everlasting covenant between God and every living creature of all flesh that is upon the earth." [17]God said to Noah, "This is the sign of the covenant which I have established between me and all flesh that is upon the earth."

L Genesis 22:1–18

[1]After these things God tested Abraham, and said to him, "Abraham!" And he said, "Here am I." God said, "Take your son, your only son Isaac, whom you love, and go to the land of Moriah, and offer him there as a burnt offering upon one of the mountains of which I shall tell you." So Abraham rose early in the morning, saddled his donkey, and took two of his servants with him, and his son Isaac; and he cut the wood for the burnt offering, and arose and went to the place of which God had told him. On the third day Abraham lifted up his eyes and saw the place afar off. Then Abraham said to his servants, "Stay here with the donkey; I and the lad will go yonder and wor-

ship, and come again to you." And Abraham took the wood of the burnt offering, and laid it on Isaac his son; and he took in his hand the fire and the knife. So they went both of them together. And Isaac said to his father Abraham, "My father!" And he said, "Here am I, my son." Isaac said, "Behold, the fire and the wood; but where is the lamb for a burnt offering?" Abraham said, "God will provide the lamb for a burnt offering to God, my son." So they went both of them together.

When they came to the place of which God had told him, Abraham built an altar there, and laid the wood in order, and bound Isaac his son, and laid him on the altar, upon the wood. Then Abraham put forth his hand, and took the knife to slay his son. But the angel of the LORD called to him from heaven, and said, "Abraham, Abraham!" And he said, "Here am I." The angel said, "Do not lay your hand on the lad or do anything to him; for now I know that you fear God, seeing you have not withheld your son, your only son, from me." And Abraham lifted up his eyes and looked, and behold, behind him was a ram, caught in a thicket by its horns; and Abraham went and took the ram, and offered it up as a burnt offering instead of his son. So Abraham called the name of that place The LORD will provide; as it is said to this day, "On the mount of the LORD it shall be provided."

And the angel of the LORD called to Abraham a second time from heaven, and said, "By myself I have sworn, says the LORD, because you have done this, and have not withheld your son, your only son, I will indeed bless you, and I will multiply your descendants as the stars of heaven and as the sand which is on the seashore. And your descendants shall possess the gate of their enemies, [18]and by your descendants shall all the nations of the earth bless themselves, because you have obeyed my voice."

SECOND READING

1 Peter 3:18–22

[18]Christ also died for sins once for all, the righteous for the unrighteous, that he might bring us to God, being put to death in the flesh but made alive in the spirit; in which he went and preached to the spirits in prison, who formerly did not obey, when God's patience waited in the days of Noah, during the building of the ark, in which a few, that is, eight persons, were saved through water. Baptism, which corresponds to this, now saves you, not as a removal of dirt from the body but as an appeal to God for a clear conscience, through the resurrection of Jesus Christ, [22]who has gone into heaven and is at the right hand of God, with angels, authorities, and powers subject to him.

L   Romans 8:31–39

[31]What then shall we say to this? If God is for us, who is against us? God did not spare God's own son, but gave him up for us all; how shall God then not give us all things, along with the Son? Who shall bring any charge against God's elect? It is God who justifies; who is to condemn? Is it Christ Jesus, who died, yes, who was raised from the dead, who is at the right hand of God, who indeed intercedes for us?

Who shall separate us from the love of Christ? Shall tribulation, or distress, or persecution, or famine, or nakedness, or peril, or sword? As it is written,

"For your sake we are being killed all the day long;
we are regarded as sheep to be slaughtered."

No, in all these things we are more than conquerors through the one who loved us. For I am sure that neither death, nor life, nor angels, nor principalities, nor things present, nor things to come, nor powers, [39]nor height, nor depth, nor anything else in all creation, will be able to separate us from the love of God in Christ Jesus our Lord.

GOSPEL

R L Mark 1:12–15
   E Mark 1:9–13

⁹In those days Jesus came from Nazareth of Galilee and was baptized by John in the Jordan. And coming up out of the water, immediately Jesus saw the heavens opened and the Spirit descending upon him like a dove; and a voice came from heaven, "You are my Son, the beloved one; with you I am well pleased."

¹²The Spirit immediately drove Jesus out into the wilderness. ¹³And Jesus was in the wilderness forty days, tempted by Satan, and was with the wild beasts; and the angels ministered to him.

¹⁴Now after John was arrested, Jesus came into Galilee, preaching the gospel of God, ¹⁵and saying, "The time is fulfilled, and the dominion of God is at hand; repent, and believe in the gospel."

FIRST READING

R Genesis 22:1–2, 9a, 10–13, 15–18
E Genesis 22:1–14

[1]After these things God tested Abraham, and said to him, "Abraham!" And he said, "Here am I." [2]God said, "Take your son, your only son Isaac, whom you love, and go to the land of Moriah, and offer him there as a burnt offering upon one of the mountains of which I shall tell you." [3]So Abraham rose early in the morning, saddled his donkey, and took two of his servants with him, and his son Isaac; and he cut the wood for the burnt offering, and arose and went to the place of which God had told him. On the third day Abraham lifted up his eyes and saw the place afar off. Then Abraham said to his servants, "Stay here with the donkey; I and the lad will go yonder and worship, and come again to you." And Abraham took the wood of the burnt offering, and laid it on Isaac his son, and he took in his hand the fire and the knife. So they went both of them together. And Isaac said to his father Abraham, "My father!" And he said, "Here am I, my son." Isaac said, "Behold, the fire and the wood; but where is the lamb for a burnt offering?" Abraham said, "God will provide the lamb for a burnt offering to God, my son." So they went both of them together.

[9a]When they came to the place of which God had told him, Abraham built an altar there, and laid the wood in order, [9b]and bound Isaac his son, and laid him on the altar, upon the wood. [10]Then Abraham put forth his hand, and took the knife to slay his son. But the angel of the LORD called to him from heaven, and said, "Abraham, Abraham!" And he said, "Here am I." The angel said, "Do not lay your hand on the lad or do anything to him; for now I know that you fear God, seeing you have not withheld your son, your only son, from me. [13]And Abraham lifted up his eyes and looked, and behold, behind him was a ram, caught in a thicket by its horns; and Abraham

went and took the ram, and offered it up as a burnt offering instead of his son. [14]So Abraham called the name of that place The Lord will provide; as it is said to this day, "On the mount of the Lord it shall be provided."

[15]And the angel of the Lord called to Abraham a second time from heaven, and said, "By myself I have sworn, says the Lord, because you have done this, and have not withheld your son, your only son, I will indeed bless you, and I will multiply your descendants as the stars of heaven and as the sand which is on the seashore. And your descendants shall possess the gate of their enemies, [18]and by your descendents shall all the nations of the earth bless themselves, because you have obeyed my voice."

L   Genesis 28:10–17

[10]Jacob left Beer-sheba, and went toward Haran. And he came to a certain place, and stayed there that night, because the sun had set. Taking one of the stones of the place, Jacob put it under his head and lay down in that place to sleep. And he dreamed that there was a ladder set up on the earth, and the top of it reached to heaven; and behold, the angels of God were ascending and descending on it! And behold, the Lord stood above it and said, "I am the Lord, the God of Abraham your father and the God of Isaac; the land on which you lie I will give to you and to your descendants; and your descendants shall be like the dust of the earth, and you shall spread abroad to the west and to the east and to the north and to the south; and by you and your descendants shall all the families of the earth bless themselves. Behold, I am with you and will keep you wherever you go, and will bring you back to this land; for I will not leave you until I have done that of which I have spoken to you." Then Jacob awoke from his sleep and said, "Surely the Lord is in this place; and I did not know it." [17]And Jacob was afraid, and said, "How awesome is this place! This is none other than the house of God, and this is the gate of heaven."

SECOND READING

R   Romans 8:31b–34
E   Romans 8:31–39

[31a]What then shall we say to this? [31b]If God is for us, who is against us? God did not spare God's own Son, but gave him up for us all; how shall God then not give us all things, along with the Son? Who shall bring any charge against God's elect? It is God who justifies; [34]who is to condemn? Is it Christ Jesus, who died, yes, who was raised from the dead, who is at the right hand of God, who indeed intercedes for us?

[35]Who shall separate us from the love of Christ? Shall tribulation, or distress, or persecution, or famine, or nakedness, or peril, or sword? As it is written,

"For your sake we are being killed all the day long;
we are regarded as sheep to be slaughtered."

No, in all these things we are more than conquerors through the one who loved us. For I am sure that neither death, nor life, nor angels, nor principalities, nor things present, nor things to come, nor powers, [39]nor height, nor depth, nor anything else in all creation, will be able to separate us from the love of God in Christ Jesus our Lord.

L   Romans 5:1–11

[1]Therefore, since we are justified by faith, we have peace with God through our Lord Jesus Christ, through whom we have obtained access to this grace in which we stand, and we rejoice in our hope of sharing the glory of God. More than that, we rejoice in our sufferings, knowing that suffering produces endurance, and endurance produces character, and character produces hope, and hope does not disappoint us, because God's love has been poured into our hearts through the Holy Spirit which has been given to us.

While we were still weak, at the right time Christ died for the ungodly. Why, one will hardly die for a righteous person—though perhaps for a good person one will dare even to die.

But God's own love is shown for us in that while we were yet sinners Christ died for us. Since, therefore, we are now justified by the blood of Christ, much more shall we be saved by him from the wrath of God. For if while we were enemies we were reconciled to God by the death of the Son of God, much more, now that we are reconciled, shall we be saved by the life of the Son of God. [11]Not only so, but we also rejoice in God through our Lord Jesus Christ, through whom we have now received our reconciliation.

GOSPEL

R Mark 9:2–10

[2]After six days Jesus took with him Peter and James and John, and led them up a high mountain apart by themselves; and he was transfigured before them, and his garments became glistening, intensely white, as no fuller on earth could bleach them. And there appeared to them Elijah with Moses; and they were talking to Jesus. And Peter said to Jesus, "Rabbi, it is well that we are here; let us make three booths, one for you and one for Moses and one for Elijah." For he did not know what to say, for they were exceedingly afraid. And a cloud overshadowed them, and a voice came out of the cloud, "This is my Son, the beloved one; listen to him." And suddenly looking around they no longer saw any one with them but Jesus only.

And as they were coming down the mountain, Jesus charged them to tell no one what they had seen, until the Man of Heaven should have risen from the dead. [10]So they kept the matter to themselves, questioning what the rising from the dead meant.

E L Mark 8:31–38

[31]Jesus began to teach them that the Man of Heaven must suffer many things, and be rejected by the elders and the chief priests and the scribes, and be killed, and after three days rise again. And Jesus said this plainly. And Peter took him, and began to rebuke him. But turning and seeing his disciples, Jesus rebuked Peter, and said, "Get behind me, Satan! For you are thinking in human terms, and not in those of God."

And Jesus called to him the multitude with his disciples, and said to them, "Those who would come after me, let them deny themselves and take up their cross and follow me. For those who would save their life will lose it; and those who would lose their life for my sake and the gospel's will save it. For what does it profit them, to gain the whole world and forfeit their life? For what can they give in return for their life? [38]For those who are ashamed of me and of my words in this adulterous and sinful generation, of them will the Man of Heaven also be ashamed, when he comes in the glory of his Father with the holy angels."

FIRST READING

R Exodus 20:1–3, 7–8, 12–17
E L Exodus 20:1–17

¹God spoke all these words, saying,

"I am the LORD your God, who brought you out of the land of Egypt, out of the house of bondage.

³"You shall have no other gods before me.

⁴"You shall not make for yourself a graven image, or any likeness of anything that is in heaven above, or that is in the earth beneath, or that is in the water under the earth; you shall not bow down to them or serve them; for I the LORD your God am a jealous God, visiting the iniquity of the parents upon the children to the third and the fourth generation of those who hate me, but showing steadfast love to thousands of those who love me and keep my commandments.

⁷"You shall not take the name of the LORD your god in vain; for the LORD will not hold guiltless one who takes in vain the divine name.

⁸"Remember the sabbath day, to keep it holy. ⁹Six days you shall labor, and do all your work; but the seventh day is a sabbath to the LORD your God; in it you shall not do any work, you, or your son, or your daughter, your manservant, or your maidservant, or your cattle, or the sojourner who is within your gates; for in six days the LORD made heaven and earth, the sea, and all that is in them, and rested the seventh day; therefore the LORD blessed the sabbath day and hallowed it.

¹²"Honor your father and your mother, that your days may be long in the land which the LORD your God gives you.

"You shall not kill.

"You shall not commit adultery.

"You shall not steal.

"You shall not bear false witness against your neighbor.

[17]"You shall not covet your neighbor's possessions: you shall not covet your neighbor's wife, or manservant, or maidservant, or ox, or ass, or anything that is your neighbor's."

SECOND READING

R L   1 Corinthians 1:22–25

[22]The Jews demand signs and Greeks seek wisdom, but we preach Christ crucified, a stumbling block to Jews and folly to Gentiles, but to those who are called, both Jews and Greeks, Christ the power of God and the wisdom of God. [25]For the foolishness of God is wiser than human wisdom, and the weakness of God is stronger than human strength.

E   Romans 7:13–25

[13]Did that which is good, then, bring death to me? By no means! It was sin, working death in me through what is good, in order that sin might be shown to be sin, and through the commandment might become sinful beyond measure. We know that the law is spiritual; but I am carnal, sold under sin.

I do not understand my own actions. For I do not do what I want, but I do the very thing I hate. Now if I do what I do not want, I agree that the law is good. So then it is no longer I that do it, but sin which dwells within me. For I know that nothing good dwells within me, that is, in my flesh. I can will what is right, but I cannot do it. For I do not do the good I want, but the evil I do not want is what I do. Now if I do what I do not want, it is no longer I that do it, but sin which dwells within me.

So I find it to be a law that when I want to do right, evil lies close at hand. For I delight in the law of God, in my inmost self, but I see in my physical body another law at war with the law of my mind and making me captive to the law of sin which dwells in my physical body. Wretched man that I am! Who will deliver me from this body of death? [25]Thanks be to God through Jesus Christ our Lord! So then, I of myself serve the law of God with my mind, but with my flesh I serve the law of sin.

GOSPEL

R John 2:13–25

E L John 2:13–22

[13]The Passover of the Jewish people was at hand, and Jesus went up to Jerusalem. In the temple he found those who were selling oxen and sheep and pigeons, and the money-changers at their business. And making a whip of cords, he drove them all, with the sheep and oxen, out of the temple; and he poured out the coins of the money-changers and overturned their tables. And Jesus told those who sold the pigeons, "Take these things away; you shall not make my Father's house a house of trade." His disciples remembered that it was written, "Zeal for your house will consume me." The Judeans then said to him, "What sign have you to show us for doing this?" Jesus answered them, "Destroy this temple, and in three days I will raise it up." The Judeans then said, "It has taken forty-six years to build this temple, and will you raise it up in three days?" But Jesus spoke of the temple of his body. [22]When therefore he was raised from the dead, his disciples remembered that he had said this; and they believed the scripture and the word which Jesus had spoken.

[23]Now when Jesus was in Jerusalem at the Passover feast, many believed in his name when they saw the signs which he did; but Jesus did not trust himself to them, [25]because he knew them all and needed no one to bear witness concerning humankind; for he himself knew what was in the human heart.

FIRST READING

R 2 Chronicles 36:14–16, 19–23
E 2 Chronicles 36:14–23

[14]All the leading priests and the people likewise were exceedingly unfaithful, following all the abominations of the nations; and they polluted the house of the LORD which had been hallowed in Jerusalem.

The LORD, the God of their forebears, persistently sent messengers to them, because the LORD had compassion on the chosen people and on the sacred house; [16]but they kept mocking God's messengers, despising God's words, and scoffing at the prophets, till the wrath of the LORD rose against the chosen people, till there was no remedy.

[17]Therefore the LORD brought up against them the king of the Chaldeans, who slew their enlisted men with the sword in the house of their sanctuary, and had no compassion on young men or virgin women, old people or aged folk; God gave them all into the king's hand. And all the vessels of the house of God, great and small, and the treasures of the house of the LORD, and the treasures of the king and of his princes, all these the king brought to Babylon. [19]And they burned the house of God, and broke down the wall of Jerusalem, and burned all its palaces with fire, and destroyed all its precious vessels. The king took into exile in Babylon those who had escaped from the sword, and they became servants to him and to his descendants until the establishment of the realm of Persia, to fulfill the word of the LORD by the mouth of Jeremiah, until the land had enjoyed its sabbaths. All the days that it lay desolate it kept sabbath, to fulfill seventy years.

Now in the first year of Cyrus king of Persia, that the word of the LORD by the mouth of Jeremiah might be accomplished, the LORD stirred up the spirit of Cyrus king of Persia so that he made a proclamation throughout all his realm and also put it in writing: [23]"Thus says Cyrus king of Persia, 'The LORD, the God of heaven, has given me all the realms of the earth, and has charged me to build a house for God at Jerusalem, which is in Judah. Those among you who are of God's people, may the LORD their God be with them. Let them go up.' "

L   Numbers 21:4–9

[4]From Mount Hor the people set out by the way to the Red Sea, to go around the land of Edom; and the people became impatient on the way. And they spoke against God and against Moses, "Why have you brought us up out of Egypt to die in the wilderness? For there is no food and no water, and we loathe this worthless food." Then the LORD sent fiery serpents among the people, and they bit the people, so that many people of Israel died. And the people came to Moses, and said, "We have sinned, for we have spoken against the LORD and against you; pray to the LORD, that the LORD take away the serpents from us." So Moses prayed for the people. And the LORD said to Moses, "Make a fiery serpent, and set it on a pole; and every one who is bitten, upon seeeing it, shall live." [9]So Moses made a bronze serpent, and set it on a pole; and if a serpent bit any man, that man would look at the bronze serpent and live.

SECOND READING

R E L   Ephesians 2:4–10

[4]Even when we were dead through our trespasses, God, who is rich in mercy, made us alive together with Christ (by grace you have been saved) out of the great love with which God loved us. With Christ God raised us up and enthroned us in the heavenly places in Christ Jesus, that in the coming ages might be shown the immeasurable riches of God's grace in kindness toward us in Christ Jesus. For by grace you have been saved through faith; and this is not your own doing, it is the gift of God—not because of works, lest any one should boast. [10]For we are God's handiwork, created in Christ Jesus for good works, which God prepared beforehand, that we should walk in them.

GOSPEL

R L   John 3:14–21

[14]As Moses lifted up the serpent in the wilderness, so must the Man of Heaven be lifted up, that whoever believes in him may have eternal life.

For God loved the world in this way, that God gave the Son, the only begotten one, that whoever believes in him should not perish but have eternal life. For God sent the Son into the world, not to condemn the world, but that through the Son the world might be saved. Those who believe in him are not condemned; those who do not believe are condemned already, because they have not believed in the name of the only Son of God. And this is the judgment, that the light has come into the world, and people loved darkness rather than light, because their deeds were evil. For all those who do evil hate the light, and do not come to the light, lest their deeds should be exposed. [21]But they who do what is true come to the light, that it may be clearly seen that their deeds have been wrought in God.

E   John 6:4–15

[4]Now the Passover, the feast of the Jewish people, was at hand. Lifting up his eyes, then, and seeing that a multitude was coming to him, Jesus said to Philip, "How are we to buy bread, so that these people may eat?" This Jesus said to test Philip, for he himself knew what he would do. Philip answered him, "Two hundred denarii would not buy enough bread for each of them to get a little." One of Jesus' disciples, Andrew, Simon Peter's brother, said to Jesus, "There is a child here who has five barley loaves and two fish; but what are they among so many?" Jesus said, "Make the people sit down." Now there was much grass in the place; so they sat down, the men numbering about five thousand. Jesus then took the loaves, and having given thanks, he distributed them to those who were seated, so also the fish, as much as they wanted. And when they had eaten their fill, Jesus told his disciples, "Gather up the fragments left over, that nothing may be lost." So they gathered them up and filled twelve baskets with fragments from the five

barley loaves, left by those who had eaten. When the people saw the sign which Jesus had done, they said, "This is indeed the prophet who is to come into the world!"

[15]Perceiving then that they were about to come and take him by force to make him king, Jesus withdrew again to the mountain by himself.

FIRST READING

R E L Jeremiah 31:31–34

[31]"Behold, the days are coming, says the LORD, when I will make a new covenant with the house of Israel and the house of Judah, not like the covenant which I made with their forebears when I took them by the hand to bring them out of the land of Egypt, my covenant which they broke, though I was married to them, says the LORD. But this is the covenant which I will make with the house of Israel after those days, says the LORD:
I will put my law within them, and I will write it upon their hearts; and I will be their God, and they shall be my people. [34]And no longer shall they, each of them, teach their neighbor and their kin, saying, 'Know the LORD,' for they shall all know me, from the least to them to the greatest, says the LORD; for I will forgive their iniquity, and I will remember their sin no more."

SECOND READING

R L Hebrews 5:7–9
E Hebrews 5:5–10

[5]Christ did not exalt himself to be made a high priest, but was appointed by the one who said to him,

"You are my Son,
today I have begotten you";

as God says also in another place,

"You are a priest for ever,
after the order of Melchizedek."

[7]In the days of his flesh, Jesus offered up prayers and supplications, with loud cries and tears, to the one who was able to save him from death, and for being God-fearing Jesus was heard. Although being a Son, Jesus learned obedience through what he suffered; [9]and being made perfect Jesus became the

source of eternal salvation to all who obey him, [10]being designated by God a high priest after the order of Melchizedek.

GOSPEL

John 12:20–33

[20]Among those who went up to worship at the feast were some Greeks. So these came to Philip, who was from Bethsaida in Galilee, and said to him, "Sir, we wish to see Jesus." Philip went and told Andrew; Andrew went with Philip and they told Jesus. And Jesus answered them, "The hour has come for the Man of Heaven to be glorified. Truly, truly, I say to you, unless a grain of wheat falls into the earth and dies, it remains alone; but if it dies, it bears much fruit. They who love their life lose it, and they who hate their life in this world will keep it for eternal life. Those who serve me must follow me; and where I am, there shall my servants be also; those who serve me, the Father will honor.

"Now is my soul troubled. And what shall I say? 'Father, save me from this hour'? No, for this purpose I have come to this hour. Father, glorify your name." Then a voice came from heaven, "I have glorified it, and I will glorify it again." The crowd standing by heard it and said that it had thundered. Others said, "An angel has spoken to him." Jesus answered, "This voice has come for your sake, not for mine. Now is the judgment of this world, now shall the ruler of this world be cast out; and I, when I am lifted up from the earth, will draw the whole world to myself." [33]Jesus said this to show by what death he was to die.

R E L LITURGY OF THE PALMS

R L Mark 11:1–10
E Mark 11:1–11a

[1]When Jesus and his disciples drew near to Jerusalem, to Bethphage and Bethany, at the Mount of Olives, Jesus sent two of his disciples, and said to them, "Go into the village opposite you, and immediately as you enter it you will find a colt tied, on which no one has ever sat; untie it and bring it. If any one says to you, 'Why are you doing this?' say, 'The Lord has need of it and will send it back here immediately.' " And they went away, and found a colt tied at the door out in the open street; and they untied it. And those who stood there said to them, "What are you doing, untying the colt?" And the disciples told them what Jesus had said; and they let them go. And they brought the colt to Jesus, and threw their garments on it; and he sat upon it. And many spread their garments on the road, and others spread leafy branches which they had cut from the fields. And those who went before and those who followed cried out, "Hosanna! Blessed is the one who comes in the name of the Lord! [10]Blessed is the coming dominion of our father David! Hosanna in the highest!"

[11a]And Jesus entered Jerusalem, and went into the temple.

FIRST READING

R Isaiah 50:4–7

⁴The Lord GOD has given me
  the tongue of those who are taught,
that I may know how to sustain with a word
  those who are weary.
Morning by morning the Lord GOD wakens,
  wakens my ear,
    to hear as those who are taught.
The Lord GOD has opened my ear,
  and I was not rebellious,
    I turned not backward.
I gave my back to the smiters,
  and my cheeks to those who pulled out the beard;
I hid not my face
  from shame and spitting.
⁷For the Lord GOD helps me;
  therefore I have not been confounded;
therefore I have set my face like a flint,
  and I know that I shall not be put to shame.

E Isaiah 45:21–25

[Thus says the LORD:]

²¹"Declare and present your case;
  let them take counsel together!
Who told this long ago?
  Who declared it of old?
Was it not I, the LORD?
  And there is no other god besides me,
a righteous God and a Savior;
  there is none besides me.
Turn to me and be saved,
  all the ends of the earth!
  For I am God, and there is no other.
By myself I have sworn,

from my mouth has gone forth in righteousness
    a word that shall not return:
'To me every knee shall bow,
    every tongue shall swear.'
Only in the LORD, it shall be said of me,
    are righteousness and strength;
to the LORD shall come and be ashamed,
    all who were incensed against God.
²⁵In the LORD all the offspring of Israel
    shall triumph and glory."

L   Zechariah 9:9–10

⁹Rejoice greatly, O daughter Zion!
    Shout aloud, O daughter Jerusalem!
Lo, your king comes to you;
    triumphant and victorious is he,
humble and riding on a donkey,
    on a colt the foal of a donkey.
¹⁰I will cut off the chariot from Ephraim
    and the war horse from Jerusalem;
and the battle bow shall be cut off,
    and the king shall command peace to the nations;
his dominion shall be from sea to sea,
    and from the River to the ends of the earth.

SECOND READING

R   Philippians 2:6–11
E L   Philippians 2:5–11

⁵Have this mind among yourselves, which is yours in Christ
Jesus, ⁶who, being in the form of God, did not count equality
with God a thing to be grasped, but gave it up, taking the form
of a servant, being born in human likeness. And being found in
human form he humbled himself and became obedient unto
death, even death on a cross. Therefore God has highly exalted
him and bestowed on him the name which is above every
name, that at the name of Jesus every knee should bow, in
heaven and on earth and under the earth, ¹¹and every tongue

confess that Jesus Christ is Lord, to the glory of God, the Father.

GOSPEL

R L   Mark 14:1–15:47
   E   Mark 15:1–39

Speaking parts:

Narrator
Jesus
Speaker: Peter, Judas, High Priest, Maid, Pilate, Bystander, Centurion, People

Narrator:
¹It was now two days before the Passover and the feast of Unleavened Bread. And the chief priests and the scribes were seeking how to arrest Jesus by stealth, and kill him; for they said,

People:
Not during the feast, lest there be a tumult of the people.

Narrator:
And while Jesus was at Bethany in the house of Simon the leper as he sat at table, a woman came with an alabaster flask of ointment of pure nard, very costly, and she broke the flask and poured it over Jesus' head. But there were some who said to themselves indignantly,

People:
Why was the ointment thus wasted? For this ointment might have been sold for more than three hundred denarii, and given to the poor.

Narrator:
And they reproached her. But Jesus said,

Jesus:
Let her alone, why do you trouble her? She has done a beautiful thing to me. For you always have the poor with you, and whenever you will, you can do good to them; but you will not

always have me. She has done what she could; she has anointed my body beforehand for burying. And truly, I say to you, wherever the gospel is preached in the whole world, what she has done will be told in memory of her.

Narrator:
Then Judas Iscariot, who was one of the twelve, went to the chief priests in order to betray Jesus to them. And when they heard it they were glad, and promised to give Judas money. And he sought an opportunity to betray Jesus. And on the first day of Unleavened Bread, when they sacrificed the passover lamb, Jesus' disciples said to him,

People:
Where will you have us go and prepare for you to eat the passover?

Narrator:
And Jesus sent two of his disciples, and said to them,

Jesus:
Go into the city, and someone carrying a jar of water will meet you; follow him, and wherever he enters, say to the householder, "The Teacher says, Where is my guest room, where I am to eat the passover with my disciples?" The householder will show you a large upper room furnished and ready; there prepare for us.

Narrator:
And the disciples set out and went to the city, and found it as Jesus had told them; and they prepared the passover. And when it was evening he came with the twelve. And as they were at table eating, Jesus said,

Jesus:
Truly, I say to you, one of you will betray me, one who is eating with me.

Narrator:
They began to be sorrowful, and to say to him one after another,

People:
Is it I?

Narrator:
He said to them,

Jesus:
It is one of the twelve, one who is dipping bread into the dish with me. For the Man of Heaven goes as it is written of him, but woe to that person by whom the Man of Heaven is betrayed! It would have been better for that person if he had not been born.

Narrator:
And as they were eating, Jesus took bread, and blessed, and broke it, and gave it to them, and said,

Jesus:
Take; this is my body.

Narrator:
And he took a cup, and having given thanks he gave it to them, and they all drank of it. And he said to them,

Jesus:
This is my blood of the covenant, which is poured out for many. Truly, I say to you, I shall not drink again of the fruit of the vine until that day when I drink it new in the dominion of God.

Narrator:
And when they had sung a hymn, they went out to the Mount of Olives. And Jesus said to them,

Jesus:
You will all fall away; for it is written, "I will strike the shepherd, and the sheep will be scattered." But after I am raised up, I will go before you to Galilee.

Narrator:
Peter said to him,

Peter:
Even though they all fall away, I will not.

Narrator:
And Jesus said to him,

Jesus:
Truly, I say to you, this very night, before the cock crows twice, you will deny me three times.

Narrator:
But Peter said vehemently,

Peter:
If I must die with you, I will not deny you.

Narrator:
And they all said the same.

And they went to a place which was called Gethsemane; and Jesus said to his disciples,

Jesus:
Sit here, while I pray.

Narrator:
And Jesus took with him Peter and James and John, and began to be greatly distressed and troubled. And he said to them,

Jesus:
My soul is very sorrowful, even to death; remain here, and watch.

Narrator:
And going a little farther, he fell on the ground and prayed that, if it were possible, the hour might pass from him. And he said,

Jesus:
Abba, Father, all things are possible to you; remove this cup from me; yet not what I will, but what you will.

Narrator:
And Jesus came and found them sleeping, and said to Peter,

Jesus:
Simon, are you asleep? Could you not watch one hour? Watch and pray that you may not enter into temptation; the spirit indeed is willing, but the flesh is weak.

Narrator:
And again Jesus went away and prayed, saying the same words. And again he came and found them sleeping, for their

eyes were very heavy; and they did not know what to answer him. And he came the third time, and said to them,

Jesus:
Are you still sleeping and taking your rest? It is enough; the hour has come; the Man of Heaven is betrayed into the hands of sinners. Rise, let us be going; see, my betrayer is at hand.

Narrator:
And immediately, while Jesus was still speaking, Judas came, one of the twelve, and with him a crowd with swords and clubs, from the chief priests and the scribes and the elders. Now the betrayer had given them a sign, saying,

Judas:
Whomever I shall kiss is the one; seize him and lead him away under guard.

Narrator:
And when Judas came, he went up to Jesus at once, and said,

Judas:
Master!

Narrator:
And he kissed him. And they laid hands on Jesus and seized him. But one of those who stood by drew his sword, and struck the slave of the high priest and cut off his ear. And Jesus said to them,

Jesus:
Have you come out as against a robber, with swords and clubs to capture me? Day after day I was with you in the temple teaching, and you did not seize me. But let the scriptures be fulfilled.

Narrator:
And they all forsook him and fled.

And a young man followed Jesus with nothing but a linen cloth about his body; and they seized him, but he left the linen cloth and ran away naked.

And they led Jesus to the high priest; and all the chief priests and the elders and the scribes were assembled.

And Peter had followed him at a distance, right into the courtyard of the high priest, and was sitting with the guards, warming himself at the fire. Now the chief priests and the whole
council sought testimony against Jesus to put him to death; but
they found none. For many bore false witness against Jesus and
their witness did not agree. And some stood up and bore false
witness against him, saying,

People:
We heard him say, "I will destroy this temple that is made with
hands, and in three days I will build another, not made with
hands."

Narrator:
Yet not even so did their testimony agree. And the high priest
stood up in the midst, and asked Jesus,

High Priest:
Have you no answer to make? What is it that these people testify against you?

Narrator:
But Jesus was silent and made no answer. Again the high
priest asked him,

High Priest:
Are you the Christ, the Son of the Blessed?

Narrator:
And Jesus said,

Jesus:
I am; and you will see the Man of Heaven seated at the right
hand of Power, and coming with the clouds of heaven.

Narrator:
And the high priest tore his garments, and said,

High Priest:
Why do we still need witnesses? You have heard his blasphemy. What is your decision?

Narrator:
And they all condemned him as deserving death. And some
began to spit on him, and to cover his face, and to strike him,

saying to him, "Prophesy!" And the guards received him with blows.

And as Peter was below in the courtyard, one of the maids of the high priest came, and seeing Peter warming himself, she looked at him, and said,

Maid:
You also were with the Nazarene, Jesus.

Narrator:
But he denied it, saying,

Peter:
I neither know nor understand what you mean.

Narrator:
And Peter went out into the gateway. And the maid saw him, and began again to say to the bystanders,

Maid:
This man is one of them.

Narrator:
But again he denied it. And after a little while again the by-standers said to Peter,

People:
Certainly you are one of them; for you are a Galilean.

Narrator:
But he began to invoke a curse on himself and to swear,

Peter:
I do not know this one of whom you speak.

Narrator:
And immediately the cock crowed a second time. And Peter remembered how Jesus had said to him, "Before the cock crows twice, you will deny me three times."

Narrator:
And he broke down and wept.

[1]And as soon as it was morning the chief priests, with the elders and scribes, and the whole council held a consultation;

and they bound Jesus and led him away and delivered him to Pilate. And Pilate asked him,

Pilate:
Are you the King of the Jews?

Narrator:
And Jesus answered him,

Jesus:
You have said so.

Narrator:
And the chief priests accused him of many things. And Pilate again asked him,

Pilate:
Have you no answer to make? See how many charges they bring against you.

Narrator:
But Jesus made no further answer, so that Pilate wondered.

Now at the feast Pilate used to release for them one prisoner for whom they asked. And among the rebels in prison, who had committed murder in the insurrection, there was someone called Barabbas. And the crowd came up and began to ask Pilate to do as he was wont to do for them. And he answered them,

Pilate:
Do you want me to release for you the King of the Jews?

Narrator:
For he perceived that it was out of envy that the chief priests had delivered him up. But the chief priests stirred up the crowd to have Pilate release for them Barabbas instead. And Pilate again said to them,

Pilate:
Then what shall I do with the one whom you call the King of the Jews?

Narrator:
And they cried out again,

People:
Crucify him.

Narrator:
And Pilate said to them,

Pilate:
Why, what evil has he done?

Narrator:
But they shouted all the more,

People:
Crucify him.

Narrator:
So Pilate, wishing to satisfy the crowd, released for them Barabbas, and having scourged Jesus, delivered him to be crucified.

And the soldiers led Jesus away inside the palace (that is, the praetorium); and they called together the whole battalion. And they clothed him in a purple cloak, and plaiting a crown of thorns they put it on him. And they began to salute him,

People:
Hail, King of the Jews!

Narrator:
And they struck his head with a reed, and spat upon him, and they knelt down in homage to him. And when they had mocked him, they stripped him of the purple cloak, and put his own clothes on him. And they led him out to crucify him.

And they compelled a passer-by, Simon of Cyrene, who was coming in from the country, the father of Alexander and Rufus, to carry his cross. And they brought him to the place called Golgotha (which means the place of a skull). And they offered Jesus wine mingled with myrrh; but he did not take it. And they crucified him, and divided his garments among them, casting lots for them, to decide what each should take. And it was the third hour, when they crucified him. And the inscription of the charge against him read, "The King of the Jews." And with him they crucified two robbers, one on his right and one on his left. And those who passed by derided him, wagging their heads, and saying,

People:
Aha! You who would destroy the temple and build it in three days, save yourself, and come down from the cross!

Narrator:
So also the chief priests mocked him to one another with the scribes, saying,

People:
He saved others; he cannot save himself. Let the Christ, the King of Israel, come down now from the cross, that we may see and believe.

Narrator:
Those who were crucified with him also reviled him.

And when the sixth hour had come there was darkness over the whole land until the ninth hour. And at the ninth hour Jesus cried with a loud voice,

Jesus:
Eloi, Eloi, lama sabachthani?

Narrator:
which means, "My God, my God, why have you forsaken me?"

And some of the bystanders hearing it said,

People:
Behold, he is calling Elijah.

Narrator:
And one ran and, filling a sponge full of vinegar, put it on a reed and gave it to him to drink, saying,

Bystander:
Wait, let us see whether Elijah will come to take him down.

Narrator:
And Jesus uttered a loud cry, and breathed his last, And the curtain of the temple was torn in two, from top to bottom.

[39]And when the centurion, who stood facing him, saw that Jesus thus breathed his last, he said,

Centurion:
Truly this man was the Son of God!

Narrator:
[40]There were also women looking on from afar, among whom were Mary Magdalene, and Mary the mother of James the younger and of Joses, and Salome, who, when Jesus was in Galilee, followed him, and ministered to him; and also many other women who came up with Jesus to Jerusalem.

And when evening had come, since it was the day of Preparation, that is, the day before the sabbath, Joseph of Arimathea, a respected member of the council, who was also himself looking for the dominion of God, took courage and went to Pilate, and asked for the body of Jesus. And Pilate wondered if Jesus were already dead; and summoning the centurion, Pilate asked him whether he was already dead. And when Pilate learned from the centurion that Jesus was dead, he granted the dead body to Joseph. And Joseph bought a linen shroud, and taking him down, wrapped him in the linen shroud, and laid him in a tomb which had been hewn out of the rock; and Joseph rolled a stone against the door of the tomb. [47]Mary Magdalene and Mary the mother of Joses saw where he was laid.

R HOLY THURSDAY
E L MAUNDY THURSDAY

FIRST READING

R Exodus 12:1–8, 11–14
E Exodus 12:1–14a

¹The LORD said to Moses and Aaron in the land of Egypt, "This month shall be for you the beginning of months; it shall be the first month of the year for you. Tell all the congregation of Israel that on the tenth day of this month they shall take every man a lamb according to their fathers' houses, a lamb for a household; and if the household is too small for a lamb, then a man and his neighbor next to his house shall take according to the number of persons; according to what each can eat you shall make your count for the lamb. Your lamb shall be without blemish, a male a year old; you shall take it from the sheep or from the goats; and you shall keep it until the fourteenth day of this month, when the whole assembly of the congregation of Israel shall kill their lambs in the evening. Then they shall take some of the blood, and put it on the two doorposts and the lintel of the houses in which they eat them. ⁸They shall eat the flesh that night, roasted; with unleavened bread and bitter herbs they shall eat it. ⁹Do not eat any of it raw or boiled with water, but roasted, its head with its legs and its inner parts. And you shall let none of it remain until the morning, anything that remains until the morning you shall burn. ¹¹In this manner you shall eat it: your loins girded, your sandals on your feet, and your staff in your hand; and you shall eat it in haste. It is the LORD's passover. For I will pass through the land of Egypt that night, and I will smite all the first-born in the land of Egypt, both human and animal; and on all the gods of Egypt I will execute judgments: I am the LORD. The blood shall be a sign for you, upon the houses where you are; and when I see the blood, I will pass over you, and no plague shall fall upon you to destroy you, when I smite the land of Egypt.

¹⁴ᵃ"This day shall be for you a memorial day, and you shall keep it as a feast to the LORD; ¹⁴ᵇthroughout your generations you shall observe it as an ordinance for ever."

L   Exodus 24:3–11

³Moses came and told the people all the words of the LORD and all the ordinances; and all the people answered with one voice, and said, "All the words which the LORD has spoken we will do." And Moses wrote all the words of the LORD. And he rose early in the morning, and built an altar at the foot of the mountain, and twelve pillars, according to the twelve tribes of Israel. And Moses sent youths of the people of Israel, who offered burnt offerings and sacrificed peace offerings of oxen to the LORD. And Moses took half of the blood and put it in basins, and half of the blood he threw against the altar. Then he took the book of the covenant, and read it in the hearing of the people; and they said, "All that the LORD has spoken we will do, and we will be obedient." And Moses took the blood and threw it upon the people, and said, "Behold the blood of the covenant which the LORD has made with you in accordance with all these words."

Then Moses and Aaron, Nadab, and Abihu, and seventy of the elders of Israel went up, and they saw the God of Israel; and there was under God's feet as it were a pavement of sapphire stone, like the very heaven for clearness. ¹¹And the LORD did not lay a hand on the leaders of the people of Israel; they beheld God, and ate and drank.

SECOND READING

R E   1 Corinthians 11:23–26

²³For I received from the Lord what I also delivered to you, that the Lord Jesus on the night when he was betrayed took bread, and having given thanks, broke it, and said, "This is my body which is for you. Do this in remembrance of me." In the same way also the cup, after supper, saying, "This cup is the new covenant in my blood. Do this, as often as you drink it, in remembrance of me." ²⁶For as often as you eat this bread and drink the cup, you proclaim the Lord's death until he comes.

L   1 Corinthians 10:16–17

¹⁶The cup of blessing which we bless, is it not a participation
in the blood of Christ? The bread which we break, is it not a
participation in the body of Christ? ¹⁷Because there is one
bread, we who are many are one body, for we all partake of the
one bread.

GOSPEL

R E   John 13:1–15

¹Now before the feast of the Passover, when Jesus knew that
his hour had come to depart out of this world to the Father,
having loved his own who were in the world, he loved them to
the end. And during supper, when the devil had already put it
into the heart of Judas Iscariot, Simon's son, to betray him, Jesus, knowing that the Father had given all things into his
hands, and that he had come from God and was going to God,
rose from supper, laid aside his garments, and girded himself
with a towel. Then he poured water into a basin, and began to
wash the disciples' feet, and to wipe them with the towel with
which he was girded. Jesus came to Simon Peter; and Peter said
to him, "Lord, do you wash my feet?" Jesus answered him,
"What I am doing you do not know now, but afterward you
will understand." Peter said to him, "You shall never wash my
feet." Jesus answered Peter, "If I do not wash you, you have
no part in me." Simon Peter said to Jesus, "Lord, not my feet
only but also my hands and my head!" Jesus said to him,
"Those who have bathed do not need to wash, except for their
feet, but they are clean all over; and you are clean, but not
every one of you." For Jesus knew who was to betray him; that
was why he said, "You are not all clean."

When Jesus had washed their feet, and taken his garments, and
resumed his place, he said to them, "Do you know what I have
done to you? You call me Teacher and Lord; and you are right,
for so I am. If I then, your Lord and Teacher, have washed
your feet, you also ought wash one another's feet. ¹⁵For I have
given you an example, that you should do as I have done to
you."

L   Mark 14:12–26

¹²On the first day of Unleavened Bread, when they sacrificed the passover lamb, Jesus' disciples said to him, "Where will you have us go and prepare for you to eat the passover?" And Jesus sent two of his disciples, and said to them, "Go into the city, and someone carrying a jar of water will meet you; follow him, and wherever he enters, say to the householder, 'The Teacher says, Where is my guest room, where I am to eat the passover with my disciples?' The householder will show you a large upper room furnished and ready; there prepare for us." And the disciples set out and went to the city, and found it as Jesus had told them; and they prepared the passover.

And when it was evening he came with the twelve. And as they were at table eating, Jesus said, "Truly, I say to you, one of you will betray me, one who is eating with me." They began to be sorrowful, and to say to him one after another, "Is it I?" He said to them, "It is one of the twelve, one who is dipping bread into the dish with me. For the Man of Heaven goes as it is written of him, but woe to that person by whom the Man of Heaven is betrayed! It would have been better for that person if he had not been born."

And as they were eating, Jesus took bread, and blessed, and broke it, and gave it to them, and said, "Take; this is my body." And he took a cup, and having given thanks he gave it to them, and they all drank of it. And he said to them, "This is my blood of the covenant, which is poured out for many. Truly, I say to you, I shall not drink again of the fruit of the vine until that day when I drink it new in the dominion of God."

²⁶And when they had sung a hymn, they went out to the Mount of Olives.

FIRST READING

¹³Behold, my servant shall prosper,
   shall be exalted and lifted up,
   and shall be very high.
As many were astonished at the one
   whose appearance was so marred, beyond human semblance,
   and whose form was beyond that of humankind,
so shall my servant startle many nations;
   rulers shall shut their mouths because of him;
for that which has not been told them they shall see,
   and that which they have not heard they shall understand.
Who has believed what we have heard?
   And to whom has the arm of the LORD been revealed?
For the servant grew up before the LORD like a young plant,
   and like a root out of dry ground,
having no form or comeliness for us to behold,
   and no beauty for us to desire.
He was despised and rejected by men,
   a man of sorrows, and acquainted with grief;
and as one from whom people hid their faces
   he was despised, and we esteemed him not.
Surely he has borne our griefs
   and carried our sorrows;
yet we esteemed him stricken,
   smitten by God, and afflicted.
But he was wounded for our transgressions,
   and was bruised for our iniquities;
the chastisement that made us whole was upon him,
   by whose stripes we are healed.
All we like sheep have gone astray;
   we have turned each one to our own way,
and the LORD has laid on this servant
   the iniquity of us all.
This servant was oppressed and was afflicted,

yet opened not his mouth;
like a lamb that is led to the slaughter,
   and like a ewe that before her shearers is dumb,
   so he opened not his mouth.
By oppression and judgment the servant was taken away;
   and as for his generation, who considered
that he was cut off out of the land of the living,
   stricken for the transgression of my people?
He was given a grave with the wicked,
   and was with the rich in death,
although having done no violence,
   having never spoken deceit.
Yet it was the will of the LORD to bruise this servant;
   the LORD has put him to grief;
making himself an offering for sin,
   the servant shall see offspring and shall prolong his days;
the will of the LORD shall prosper in the hand of the servant,
   who shall see the fruit of the travail of his soul and be
      satisfied;
by his knowledge shall the righteous one, my servant,
   make many to be accounted righteous;
   my servant shall bear their iniquities.
[12]Therefore I will divide a portion with the great for my servant
   who shall divide the spoil with the strong;
because my servant poured out his soul to death,
   and was numbered with the transgressors;
yet he bore the sin of many,
   and made intercession for the transgressors.

SECOND READING

R L   Hebrews 4:14–16, 5:7–9

[14]Since then we have a great high priest who has passed through the heavens, Jesus, the Son of God, let us hold fast our confession. For we have not a high priest who is unable to sympathize with our weaknesses, but one who in every respect has been tempted as we are, yet without sin. [16]Let us then with confidence draw near to the throne of grace, that we may receive mercy and find grace to help in time of need.

[7]In the days of his flesh, Jesus offered up prayers and supplications, with loud cries and tears, to the one who was able to save him from death, and for being God-fearing Jesus was heard. Although being a Son, Jesus learned obedience through what he suffered; [9]and being made perfect Jesus became the source of eternal salvation to all who obey him.

E   Hebrews 10:1–25

[1]For since the law has but a shadow of the good things to come instead of the true form of these realities, it can never, by the same sacrifices which are continually offered year after year, make perfect those who draw near. Otherwise, would they not have ceased to be offered? If the worshipers had once been cleansed, they would no longer have any consciousness of sin. But in these sacrifices there is a reminder of sin year after year. For it is impossible that the blood of bulls and goats should take away sins.

Consequently, coming into the world, Christ said,

"Sacrifices and offerings you have not desired,
but a body you have prepared for me;
in burnt offerings and sin offerings you have taken no pleasure.
Then I said, 'Lo, I have come to do your will, O God,'
as it is written of me in the roll of the book."

When Christ said above, "You have neither desired nor taken pleasure in sacrifices and offerings and burnt offerings and sin offerings" (these are offered according to the law), then Christ added, "Lo, I have come to do your will." Christ abolishes the first in order to establish the second. And by that will we have been sanctified through the offering of the body of Jesus Christ once for all.

And every priest stands at the daily service, offering repeatedly the same sacrifices, which can never take away sins. But when Christ had offered for all time a single sacrifice for sins, he sat down at the right hand of God, then to wait until his enemies should be made a stool for his feet. For by a single offering

Christ has perfected for all time those who are sanctified. And the Holy Spirit also bears witness to us; for after saying,

"This is the covenant that I will make with them
after those days, says the Lord:
I will put my laws on their hearts, and write them on their
    minds,"

then is added,

"I will remember their sins and their misdeeds no more."

Where there is forgiveness of these, there is no longer any offering for sin.

Therefore, my dear people, since we have confidence to enter the sanctuary by the blood of Jesus, by the new and living way which Christ opened for us through the curtain, that is, through his flesh, and since we have a great priest over the house of God, let us draw near with a true heart in full assurance of faith, with our hearts sprinkled clean from an evil conscience and our bodies washed with pure water. Let us hold fast the confession of our hope without wavering, for the one who promised is faithful; and let us consider how to stir up one another to love and good works, [25]not neglecting to meet together, as is the habit of some, but encouraging one another, and all the more as you see the Day drawing near.

GOSPEL

R L   John 18:1–19:42
E   John 19:1–37

Narrator
Jesus
Speaker: Maid, Peter, Officer, Servant, Pilate, People

Narrator:
[1]When Jesus had spoken these words, he went forth with his disciples across the Kidron Valley, where there was a garden, which he and his disciples entered. Now Judas, who betrayed

him, also knew the place; for Jesus often met there with his disciples. So Judas, procuring a band of soldiers and some officers from the chief priests and the Pharisees, went there with lanterns and torches and weapons. Then Jesus, knowing all that was to befall him, came forward and said to them,

Jesus:
Whom do you seek?

Narrator:
They answered him,

People:
Jesus of Nazareth.

Narrator:
Jesus said to them,

Jesus:
Here I am.

Narrator:
Judas, who betrayed Jesus was standing with them. When Jesus said to them, "Here I am," they drew back and fell to the ground. Again Jesus asked them,

Jesus:
Whom do you seek?

Narrator:
And they said,

People:
Jesus of Nazareth.

Narrator:
Jesus answered,

Jesus:
I told you here I am; so, if you seek me, let these others go.

Narrator:
This was to fulfill the word which Jesus had spoken, "Of those whom you gave me I lost not one." Then Simon Peter, having a sword, drew it and struck the high priest's slave and cut off his right ear. The slave's name was Malchus. Jesus said to Peter,

Jesus:

Put your sword into its sheath; shall I not drink the cup which the Father has given me?

Narrator:

So the band of soldiers and their captain and the officers of the Judeans seized Jesus and bound him. First they led him to Annas, the father-in-law of Caiaphas, who was high priest that year. It was Caiaphas who had given counsel to the Judeans that it was expedient that one person should die for the people.

Simon Peter followed Jesus, and so did another disciple. Being known to the high priest, that disciple entered the court of the high priest along with Jesus, while Peter stood outside at the door. So the other disciple, who was known to the high priest, went out and spoke to the maid who kept the door, and brought Peter in. The maid who kept the door said to Peter,

Maid:

Are not you also one of this man's disciples?

Narrator:

He said,

Peter:

I am not.

Narrator:

Now the servants and officers had made a charcoal fire, because it was cold, and they were standing and warming themselves; Peter also was with them, standing and warming himself.

The high priest then questioned Jesus about his disciples and his teaching. Jesus answered the high priest,

Jesus:

I have spoken openly to the world; I have always taught in synagogues and in the temple, where all the Jewish people come together; I have said nothing secretly. Why do you ask me? Ask those who have heard me, what I said to them; they know what I said.

Narrator:
When he had said this, one of the officers standing by struck
Jesus with his hand, saying,

Officer:
Is that how you answer the high priest?

Narrator:
Jesus answered the officer,

Jesus:
If I have spoken wrongly, bear witness to the wrong; but if I
have spoken rightly, why do you strike me?

Narrator:
Annas then sent Jesus bound to Caiaphas the high priest. Now
Simon Peter was standing and warming himself. They said to
Peter,

People:
Are not you also one of his disciples?

Narrator:
He denied it and said,

Peter:
I am not.

Narrator:
One of the servants of the high priest, a relative of the man
whose ear Peter had cut off, asked,

Servant:
Did I not see you in the garden with him?

Narrator:
Peter again denied it; and at once the cock crowed.

Then they led Jesus from the house of Caiaphas to the
praetorium. It was early. They themselves did not enter the
praetorium, so that they might not be defiled, but might eat the
passover. So Pilate went out to them and said,

Pilate:
What accusation do you bring against this man?

Narrator:
They answered Pilate,

People:
If this man were not an evildoer, we would not have handed him over.

Narrator:
Pilate said to them,

Pilate:
Take him yourselves and judge him by your own law.

Narrator:
The Judeans said to him,

People:
It is not lawful for us to put anyone to death.

Narrator:
This was to fulfill the word which Jesus had spoken to show by what death he was to die.

Pilate entered the praetorium again and called Jesus, saying,

Pilate:
Are you the King of the Jews?

Narrator:
Jesus answered,

Jesus:
Do you say this of your own accord, or did others say it to you about me?

Narrator:
Pilate answered,

Pilate:
Am I a Jew? Your own nation and the chief priests have handed you over to me; what have you done?

Narrator:
Jesus answered,

Jesus:
My kingship is not of this world; if my kingship were of this world, my servants would fight, that I might not be handed over to the Judeans; but my kingship is not from the world.

Narrator:
Pilate said to him,

Pilate:
So you are a king?

Narrator:
Jesus answered,

Jesus:
You say that I am a king. For this I was born, and for this I have come into the world, to bear witness to the truth. Every one who is of the truth hears my voice.

Narrator:
Pilate said to Jesus,

Pilate:
What is truth?

Narrator:
Having said this, Pilate went out to the Judeans again, and told them,

Pilate:
I find no crime in him. But you have a custom that I should release one person for you at the Passover; will you have me release for you the King of the Jews?

Narrator:
They cried out again,

People:
Not this man, but Barabbas!

Narrator:
Now Barabbas was a robber.

¹Then Pilate took Jesus and scourged him. And the soldiers plaited a crown of thorns, and put it on his head, and arrayed him in a purple robe; they came up to Jesus, saying,

People:
Hail, King of the Jews!

Narrator:
and struck him with their hands. Pilate went out again, and said to them,

Pilate:

See, I am bringing him out to you, that you may know that I find no crime in him.

Narrator:

So Jesus came out, wearing the crown of thorns and the purple robe. Pilate said to them,

Pilate:

Behold the man!

Narrator:

When the chief priests and the officers saw him, they cried out,

People:

Crucify him, crucify him!

Narrator:

Pilate said to them,

Pilate:

Take him yourselves and crucify him, for I find no crime in him.

Narrator:

The Judeans answered him,

People:

We have a law, and by that law he ought to die, because he has made himself the Son of God.

Narrator:

When Pilate heard these words, he was the more afraid; he entered the praetorium again and said to Jesus,

Pilate:

Where are you from?

Narrator:

But Jesus gave no answer. Pilate therefore said to him,

Pilate:

You will not speak to me? Do you not know that I have power to release you, and power to crucify you?

Narrator:

Jesus answered him,

Jesus:
You would have no power over me unless it had been given you from above; therefore the one who delivered me to you has the greater sin.

Narrator:
Upon this Pilate sought to release him, but the Judeans cried out,

People:
If you release this man, you are not Caesar's friend; every one who makes himself a king sets himself against Caesar.

Narrator:
When Pilate heard these words, he brought Jesus out and sat down on the judgment seat at a place called The Pavement, and in Hebrew, Gabbatha. Now it was the day of the Preparation of the Passover; it was about the sixth hour. He said to the Judeans,

Pilate:
Behold your king!

Narrator:
They cried out,

People:
Away with him, away with him, crucify him!

Narrator:
Pilate said to them,

Pilate:
Shall I crucify your king?

Narrator:
The chief priests answered,

People:
We have no king but Caesar.

Narrator:
Then Pilate handed Jesus over to them to be crucified.

So they took Jesus, and he went out, bearing his own cross, to the place called the place of a skull, which is called in Hebrew Golgotha. There they crucified Jesus, and with him two others, one on either side, and Jesus between them. Pilate also wrote a title and put it on the cross; it read, "Jesus of Nazareth, the King of the Jews." Many of the Judeans read this title, for the place where Jesus was crucified was near the city; and it was written in Hebrew, in Latin, and in Greek. The chief priests of the Jewish people then said to Pilate,

People:
Do not write, "The King of the Jews," but, "This man said, I am King of the Jews."

Narrator:
Pilate answered,

Pilate:
What I have written I have written.

Narrator:
When the soldiers had crucified Jesus they took his garments and made four parts, one for each soldier; also the tunic. But the tunic was without seam, woven from top to bottom; so they said to one another,

People:
Let us not tear it, but cast lots for it to see whose it shall be.

Narrator:
This was to fulfill the scripture,

"They parted my garments among them,
and for my clothing they cast lots."

So the soldiers did this. But standing by the cross of Jesus were his mother, and his mother's sister, Mary the wife of Clopas, and Mary Magdalene. When Jesus saw his mother, and the disciple whom he loved standing near, he said to his mother,

Jesus:
Woman, behold your son!

Narrator:
Then he said to the disciple,

Jesus:
Behold, your mother!

Narrator:
And from that hour the disciple took her to his own home.
After this Jesus, knowing that all was now finished, said (to
fulfill the scripture),

Jesus:
I thirst.

Narrator:
A bowl full of vinegar stood there; so they put a sponge full of
vinegar on hyssop and held it to his mouth. Having received
the vinegar, Jesus said,

Jesus:
It is finished;

Narrator:
and with bowed head he gave over the spirit.

Since it was the day of Preparation, in order to prevent the
bodies from remaining on the cross on the sabbath (for that
sabbath was a high day), the Judeans asked Pilate that their
legs might be broken, and that they might be taken away. So
the soldiers came and broke the legs of the first, and of the
other who had been crucified with him; but when they came to
Jesus and saw that he was already dead, they did not break his
legs. But one of the soldiers pierced his side with a spear, and
at once there came out blood and water. One who saw it
whose testimony is true, and who knows that he tells the truth,
has borne witness that you also may believe. For these things
took place that the scripture might be fulfilled, "Not a bone of
him shall be broken." [37]And again another scripture says,
"They shall look upon the one whom they have pierced."

[38]After this Joseph of Arimathea, who was a disciple of Jesus,
but secretly, for fear of the Judeans, asked Pilate that he might
take away the body of Jesus, and Pilate gave him leave. So Joseph came and took away Jesus' body. Nicodemus also, who
had at first come to Jesus by night, came bringing a mixture of
myrrh and aloes, about a hundred pounds' weight. They took
the body of Jesus, and bound it in linen cloths with the spices,

as is the Jewish burial custom. Now in the place where Jesus was crucified there was a garden, and in the garden a new tomb where no one had ever been laid. [42]So because of the Jewish day of Preparation, as the tomb was close at hand, they laid Jesus there.

THE EASTER VIGIL

READING

Genesis 1:1–2:3

[1]In the beginning God created the heavens and the earth. The earth was without form and void, and darkness was upon the face of the deep; and the Spirit of God was moving over the face of the waters.

And God said, "Let there be light"; and there was light. And God saw that the light was good; and God separated the light from the darkness. God called the light Day, and the darkness God called Night. And there was evening and there was morning, one day.

And God said, "Let there be a firmament in the midst of the waters, and let it separate the waters from the waters." And God made the firmament and separated the waters which were under the firmament from the waters which were above the firmament. And it was so. And God called the firmament Heaven. And there was evening and there was morning, a second day.

And God said, "Let the waters under the heavens be gathered together into one place, and let the dry land appear." And it was so. God called the dry land Earth, and the waters that were gathered together God called Seas. And God saw that it was good. And God said, "Let the earth put forth vegetation, plants yielding seed, and fruit trees bearing fruit in which is their seed, each according to its kind, upon the earth." And it was so. The earth brought forth vegetation, plants yielding seed according to their own kinds, and trees bearing fruit in which is their seed, each according to its kind. And God saw that it was good. And there was evening and there was morning, a third day.

And God said, "Let there be lights in the firmament of the heavens to separate the day from the night; and let them be for signs and for seasons and for days and years, and let them be lights in the firmament of the heavens to give light upon the earth." And it was so. And God made the two great lights, the greater light to rule the day, and the lesser light to rule the night; God made the stars also. And God set them in the firmament of the heavens to give light upon the earth, to rule over the day and over the night, and to separate the light from the darkness. And God saw that it was good. And there was evening and there was morning, a fourth day.

And God said, "Let the waters bring forth swarms of living creatures, and let birds fly above the earth across the firmament of the heavens." So God created the great sea monsters and every living creature that moves, with which the waters swarm, according to their kinds, and every winged bird according to its kind. And God saw that it was good. And God blessed them, saying, "Be fruitful and multiply and fill the waters in the seas, and let birds multiply on the earth." And there was evening and there was morning, a fifth day.

And God said, "Let the earth bring forth living creatures according to their kinds: cattle and creeping things and beasts of the earth according to their kinds." And it was so. And God made the beasts of the earth according to their kinds and the cattle according to their kinds, and everything that creeps upon the ground according to its kind. And God saw that it was good.

Then God said, "Let us make humankind in our image, after our likeness; and let them have dominion over the fish of the sea, and over the birds of the air, and over the cattle, and over all the earth, and over every creeping thing that creeps upon the earth." So God created humankind in the divine image; in the image of God humankind was created; male and female God created them. And God blessed them, and God said to them, "Be fruitful and multiply, and fill the earth and subdue it; and have dominion over the fish of the sea and over the birds of the air and over every living thing that moves upon the earth." And God said, "Behold, I have given you every plant yielding seed which is upon the face of all the earth, and every tree with seed in its fruit; you shall have them for food.

And to every beast of the earth, and to every bird of the air, and to everything that creeps on the earth, everything that has the breath of life, I have given every green plant for food." And it was so. And God saw everything that had been made, and behold, it was very good. And there was evening and there was morning, a sixth day.

Thus the heavens and the earth were finished, and all the host of them. And on the seventh day God finished the work which had been done, and God rested on the seventh day from all the work which God had done. ³So God blessed the seventh day and hallowed it, because on it God rested from all the work which God had done in creation.

READING

Genesis 7:1–5, 11–18, 8:6–18, 9:8–13

¹The LORD said to Noah, "Go into the ark, you and all your household, for I have seen that you are righteous before me in this generation. Take with you seven pairs of all clean animals, the male and his mate; and a pair of the animals that are not clean, the male and his mate; and seven pairs of the birds of the air also, male and female, to keep their kind alive upon the face of all the earth. For in seven days I will send rain upon the earth forty days and forty nights; and every living thing that I have made I will blot out from the face of the ground." ⁵And Noah did all that the LORD had commanded him.

¹¹In the six hundredth year of Noah's life, in the second month, on the seventeenth day of the month, on that day all the fountains of the great deep burst forth, and the windows of the heavens were opened. And rain fell upon the earth forty days and forty nights. On the very same day Noah and his sons, Shem and Ham and Japheth, and Noah's wife and the three wives of his sons with them entered the ark, they and every beast according to its kind, and all the cattle according to their kinds, and every creeping thing that creeps on the earth according to its kind, and every bird according to its kind, every bird of every sort. They went into the ark with Noah, two and two of all flesh in which there was the breath of life. And they that entered, male and female of all flesh, went in as God had commanded Noah; and the LORD shut him in.

The flood continued forty days upon the earth; and the waters increased, and bore up the ark, and it rose high above the earth. [18]The waters prevailed and increased greatly upon the earth; and the ark floated on the face of the waters.

[6]At the end of forty days Noah opened the window of the ark which he had made, and sent forth a raven; and it went to and fro until the waters were dried up from the earth. Then he sent forth a dove from him, to see if the waters had subsided from the face of the ground; but the dove found no place to set its foot, and it returned to him to the ark, for the waters were still on the face of the whole earth. So Noah put forth his hand and took the dove and brought it into the ark with him. He waited another seven days, and again he sent forth the dove out of the ark; and the dove came back to him in the evening, and lo, in its mouth a freshly plucked olive leaf; so Noah knew that the waters had subsided from the earth. Then he waited another seven days, and sent forth the dove; and it did not return to him any more.

In the six hundred and first year, in the first month, the first day of the month, the waters were dried from off the earth; and Noah removed the covering of the ark, and looked, and behold, the face of the ground was dry. In the second month, on the twenty-seventh day of the month, the earth was dry. Then God said to Noah, "Go forth from the ark, you and your wife, and your sons and your sons' wives with you. Bring forth with you every living thing that is with you of all flesh—birds and animals and every creeping thing that creeps on the earth—that they may breed abundantly on the earth, and be fruitful and multiply upon the earth." [18]So Noah went forth, and his sons and his wife and his sons' wives with him.

[8]Then God said to Noah and to his sons with him, "Behold, I establish my covenant with you and your descendants after you, and with every living creature that is with you, the birds, the cattle, and every beast of the earth with you, as many as came out of the ark. I establish my covenant with you, that never again shall all flesh be cut off by the waters of a flood, and never again shall there be a flood to destroy the earth."

And God said, "This is the sign of the covenant which I make between me and you and every living creature that is with you, for all future generations; ¹³I set my bow in the cloud, and it shall be a sign of the covenant between me and the earth."

READING

Genesis 22:1–18

¹After these things God tested Abraham, and said to him, "Abraham!" And he said, "Here am I." God said, "Take your son, your only son Isaac, whom you love, and go to the land of Moriah, and offer him there as a burnt offering upon one of the mountains of which I shall tell you." So Abraham rose early in the morning, saddled his donkey, and took two of his servants with him, and his son Isaac; and he cut the wood for the burnt offering, and arose and went to the place of which God had told him. On the third day Abraham lifted up his eyes and saw the place afar off. Then Abraham said to his servants, "Stay here with the donkey; I and the lad will go yonder and worship, and come again to you." And Abraham took the wood of the burnt offering, and laid it on Isaac his son; and he took in his hand the fire and the knife. So they went both of them together. And Isaac said to his father Abraham, "My father!" And he said, "Here am I, my son." Isaac said, "Behold, the fire and the wood; but where is the lamb for a burnt offering?" Abraham said, "God will provide the lamb for a burnt offering to God, my son." So they went both of them together.

When they came to the place of which God had told him, Abraham built an altar there, and laid the wood in order, and bound Isaac his son, and laid him on the altar, upon the wood. Then Abraham put forth his hand, and took the knife to slay his son. But the angel of the LORD called to him from heaven, and said, "Abraham, Abraham!" And he said, "Here am I." The angel said, "Do not lay your hand on the lad or do anything to him; for now I know that you fear God, seeing you have not withheld your son, your only son, from me." And Abraham lifted up his eyes and looked, and behold, behind him was a ram, caught in a thicket by its horns; and Abraham went and took the ram, and offered it up as a burnt offering instead of his son. So Abraham called the name of that place The LORD will provide; as it is said to this day, "On the mount of the LORD it shall be provided."

And the angel of the LORD called to Abraham a second time from heaven, and said, "By myself I have sworn, says the LORD, because you have done this, and have not withheld your son, your only son, I will indeed bless you, and I will multiply your descendants as the stars of heaven and as the sand which is on the seashore. And your descendants shall possess the gate of their enemies, [18]and by your descendants shall all the nations of the earth bless themselves, because you have obeyed my voice."

READING

Exodus 12:1–14

[1]The LORD said to Moses and Aaron in the land of Egypt, "This month shall be for you the beginning of months; it shall be the first month of the year for you. Tell all the congregation of Israel that on the tenth day of this month they shall take every man a lamb according to their fathers' houses, a lamb for a household; and if the household is too small for a lamb, then a man and his neighbor next to his house shall take according to the number of persons; according to what each can eat you shall make your count for the lamb. Your lamb shall be without blemish, a male a year old; you shall take it from the sheep or from the goats; and you shall keep it until the fourteenth day of this month, when the whole assembly of the congregation of Israel shall kill their lambs in the evening. Then they shall take some of the blood, and put it on the two doorposts and the lintel of the houses in which they eat them. They shall eat the flesh that night, roasted; with unleavened bread and bitter herbs they shall eat it. Do not eat any of it raw or boiled with water, but roasted, its head with its legs and its inner parts. And you shall let none of it remain until the morning, anything that remains until the morning you shall burn. In this manner you shall eat it; your loins girded, your sandals on your feet,

and your staff in your hand; and you shall eat it in haste. It is the LORD's passover. For I will pass through the land of Egypt that night, and I will smite all the first-born in the land of Egypt, both human and animal; and on all the gods of Egypt I will execute judgments: I am the LORD. The blood shall be a sign for you, upon the houses where you are; and when I see the blood, I will pass over you, and no plagues shall fall upon you to destroy you, when I smite the land of Egypt.

14"This day shall be for you a memorial day, and you shall keep it as a feast to the LORD; throughout your generations you shall observe it as an ordinance for ever."

READING

Exodus 14:10–15:1

10When the Pharoah drew near, the people of Israel lifted up their eyes, and behold, the Egyptians were marching after them; and they were in great fear. And the people of Israel cried out to the LORD; and they said to Moses, "Is it because there are no graves in Egypt that you have taken us away to die in the wilderness? What have you done to us, in bringing us out of Egypt? Is not this what we said to you in Egypt, 'Let us alone and let us serve the Egyptians'? For it would have been better for us to serve the Egyptians than to die in the wilderness." And Moses said to the people, "Fear not, stand firm, and see the salvation of the LORD, which the LORD will work for you today; for the Egyptians whom you see today, you shall never see again. The LORD will fight for you, and you have only to be still." The LORD said to Moses, "Why do you cry to me? Tell the people of Israel to go forward. Lift up your rod, and stretch out your hand over the sea and divide it, that the people of Israel may go on dry ground through the sea. And I will harden the hearts of the Egyptians so that they shall go in after them, and I will get glory over Pharoah and all his host, his chariots, and his horsemen. And the Egyptians shall know that I am the LORD, when I have gotten glory over Pharoah, his chariots, and his horsemen."

Then the angel of God who went before the host of Israel moved and went behind them; and the pillar of cloud moved from before them and stood behind them, coming between the host of Egypt and the host of Israel. And there was the cloud and the darkness; and the night passed without one coming near the other all night.

Then Moses stretched out his hand over the sea; and the LORD drove the sea back by a strong east wind all night, and made the sea dry land, and the waters were divided. And the people of Israel went into the midst of the sea on dry ground, the waters being a wall to them on their right hand and on their left. The Egyptians pursued, and went in after them into the midst of the sea, all Pharoah's horses, his chariots, and his horsemen. And in the morning watch the LORD in the pillar of fire and of cloud looked down upon the host of the Egyptians, and discomfited the host of the Egyptians, clogging their chariot wheels so that they drove heavily; and the Egyptians said, "Let us flee from before Israel; for the LORD fights for them against the Egyptians."

Then the LORD said to Moses, "Stretch out your hand over the sea, that the water may come back upon the Egyptians, upon their chariots, and upon their horsemen." So Moses stretched forth his hand over the sea, and the sea returned to its wonted flow when the morning appeared; and the Egyptians fled into it, and the LORD routed the Egyptians in the midst of the sea. The waters returned and covered the chariots and the horsemen and all the host of Pharoah that had followed them into the sea; not so much as one of them remained. But the people of Israel walked on dry ground through the sea, the waters being a wall to them on their right hand and on their left.

Thus the LORD saved Israel that day from the hand of the Egyptians; and Israel saw the Egyptians dead upon the seashore. And Israel saw the great work which the LORD did against the Egyptians, and the people feared the LORD; and they believed in the LORD and in Moses, the servant of the LORD.

'Then Moses and the people of Israel sang this song to the LORD, saying,

"I will sing to the LORD who has triumphed gloriously;
the horse and its rider have been thrown into the sea."

READING

Isaiah 4:2–6

²In that day the branch of the LORD shall be beautiful and glorious, and the fruit of the land shall be the pride and glory of the survivors of Israel. And whoever is left in Zion and remains in Jerusalem will be called holy, every one who has been recorded for life in Jerusalem, when the Lord shall have washed away the filth of the people of Zion and cleansed the bloodstains of Jerusalem from its midst by a spirit of judgment and by a spirit of burning. Then the LORD will create over the whole site of Mount Zion and over its assemblies a cloud by day, and smoke and the shining of a flaming fire by night; for over all the glory there will be a canopy and a pavilion. ⁶It will be for a shade by day from the heat, and for a refuge and a shelter from the storm and rain.

READING

Isaiah 55:1–11

¹"Ho, every one who thirsts,
  come to the waters;
and whoever has no money,
  come, buy and eat!
Come, buy wine and milk
  without money and without price.
Why do you spend your money for that which is not bread,
  and your labor for that which does not satisfy?
Hearken diligently to me, and eat what is good,
  and delight yourselves in fatness.
Incline your ear, and come to me;
  hear, that your soul may live;
and I will make with you an everlasting covenant,
  my steadfast, sure love for David.
Behold, I made him a witness to the peoples,

a leader and commander for the peoples.
Behold, you shall call nations that you know not,
    and nations that knew you not shall run to you,
because of the LORD your God, and of the Holy One of Israel,
    for the LORD has glorified you.
Seek the LORD while the LORD may be found,
    call upon God, while God is near;
let the wicked forsake their ways,
    and the unrighteous their thoughts;
let them return to the LORD, who will have mercy on them,
    and to our God, who will abundantly pardon.
For my thoughts are not your thoughts,
    neither are your ways my ways, says the LORD.
For as the heavens are higher than the earth,
    so are my ways higher than your ways
    and my thoughts than your thoughts.
For as the rain and the snow come down from heaven,
    and return not thither but water the earth,
making it bring forth and sprout,
    giving seed to the sower and bread to the eater,
[11]so shall my word be that goes forth from my mouth;
    it shall not return to me empty,
but it shall accomplish that which I purpose,
    and prosper in the thing for which I sent it."

READING

Ezekiel 37:1–14

[1]The hand of the LORD was upon me, and brought me out by the Spirit of the LORD, and set me down in the midst of the valley; it was full of bones. And the LORD led me round among them; and behold, there were very many upon the valley; and lo, they were very dry. And the LORD said to me, "O human one, can these bones live?" And I answered, "O Lord GOD, you know." Again the LORD said to me, "Prophesy to these bones, and say to them, O dry bones, hear the word of the LORD. Thus says the Lord GOD to these bones: Behold, I will cause breath to enter you, and you shall live. And I will lay sinews

upon you, and will cause flesh to come upon you, and cover you with skin, and put breath in you, and you shall live; and you shall know that I am the Lord."

So I prophesied as I was commanded; and as I prophesied, there was a noise, and behold, a rattling; and the bones came together, bone to its bone. And as I looked, there were sinews on them, and flesh had come upon them, and skin had covered them; but there was no breath in them. Then the Lord said to me, "Prophesy to the breath, prophesy, O human one, and say to the breath, Thus says the Lord God: Come from the four winds, O breath, and breathe upon these slain, that they may live." So I prophesied as the Lord commanded me, and the breath came into them, and they lived, and stood upon their feet, an exceedingly great host.

Then the Lord said to me, "O human one, these bones are the whole house of Israel. Behold, they say, 'Our bones are dried up, and our hope is lost; we are clean cut off.' Therefore prophesy, and say to them, Thus says the Lord God: Behold, I will open your graves, and raise you from your graves, O my people; and I will bring you home into the land of Israel. And you shall know that I am the Lord, when I open your graves, and raise you from your graves, O my people. [14]And I will put my Spirit within you, and you shall live, and I will place you in your own land; then you shall know that I, the Lord, have spoken, and I have done it, says the Lord."

READING

Baruch 3:9–4:4

[9]Hear the commandments of life, O Israel;
   give ear, and learn wisdom!
Why is it, O Israel, why is it that you are in the land of your enemies,
   that you are growing old in a foreign country,
that you are defiled with the dead,
   that you are counted among those in Hades?
You have forsaken the fountain of wisdom.

If you had walked in the way of God,
   you would be dwelling in peace for ever.
Learn where there is wisdom,
   where there is strength,
   where there is understanding,
that you may at the same time discern
   where there is length of days, and life,
   where there is light for the eyes, and peace.
Who has found the place of Wisdom?
   And who has entered her storehouses?
Where are the rulers of the nations,
   and those who govern the beasts of the earth,
those who have sport with the birds of the air,
   and who hoard up silver and gold,
in which people trust,
   and there is no end to their getting;
those who scheme to get silver, and are anxious,
   whose labors are beyond measure?
They have vanished and gone down to Hades,
   and others have arisen in their place.
Youths have seen the light of day,
   and have dwelt upon the earth;
but they have not learned the way to knowledge,
   nor understood her paths,
   nor laid hold of her.
Their children have strayed far from her way.
She has not been heard of in Canaan,
   nor seen in Teman;
the children of Hagar, who seek for understanding on the
      earth,
   the merchants of Merran and Teman,
   the story-tellers and the seekers for understanding,
have not learned the way to Wisdom,
   nor given thought to her paths.
O Israel, how great is the house of God!
   and how vast the territory that God possesses!
It is great and has no bounds;
   it is high and immeasurable.

The giants were born there, who were famous of old,
    great in stature, expert in war.
God did not choose them,
    nor give them the way to knowledge;
so they perished because they had no wisdom,
    they perished through their folly.
Who has gone up into heaven, and taken her,
    and brought her down from the clouds?
Who has gone over the sea, and found her,
    and will buy her for pure gold?
No one knows the way to her,
    or is concerned about the path to her.
But the one who knows all things knows her,
    and found her through understanding.
The one who prepared the earth for all time
    filled it with four-footed creatures;
the one who sends forth the light, and it goes,
    called it, and it hearkened in fear;
the stars shone in their watches, and were glad;
    God called them, and they said, "Here we are!"
    They shone with gladness for the one who made them.
This is our God,
    with whom none other can be compared.
God found the whole way to knowledge,
    and gave her to Jacob, God's servant,
    and to Israel, the one whom God loved.
Afterward she appeared upon earth
    and lived among humankind.
She is the book of the commandments of God,
    and the law that endures for ever.
All who hold her fast will live,
    and those who forsake her will die.
Turn, O Jacob, and take her;
    walk toward the shining of her light.
Do not give your glory to another,
    or your advantages to an alien people.
[4]Happy are we, O Israel,
    for we know what is pleasing to God.

READING

Romans 6:3–11

[3]Do you not know that all of us who have been baptized into Christ Jesus were baptized into his death? We were buried therefore with Christ by baptism into death, so that as Christ was raised from the dead by the glory of the Father, we too might walk in newness of life.

For if we have been united with Christ in a death like his, we shall certainly be united with him in a resurrection like his. We know that our old self was crucified with Christ so that the sinful body might be destroyed, and we might no longer be enslaved to sin. For whoever has died is freed from sin. But if we have died with Christ, we believe that we shall also live with him. For we know that Christ being raised from the dead will never die again; death no longer has dominion over him. The death he died he died to sin, once for all, but the life he lives he lives to God. [11]So you also must consider yourselves dead to sin and alive to God in Christ Jesus.

L   1 Corinthians 15:19–28

[19]If for this life only we have hoped in Christ, we are of all humankind most to be pitied.

But in fact Christ has been raised from the dead, the first fruits of those who have fallen asleep. For as by a human being came death, by a human being has come also the resurrection of the dead. For as in Adam all die, so also in Christ shall all be made alive. But each in the corresponding order: Christ the first fruits, then at his coming those who belong to Christ. Then comes the end, when Christ delivers the dominion to God, the Father, after destroying every rule and every authority and power. For Christ must reign until he has put all his enemies under his feet. The last enemy to be destroyed is death. "For God has put all things in subjection under the feet of him." But when it says, "All things are put in subjection under him," it is plain that the one is excepted who put all things under him. [28]When all things are subjected to Christ, then the Son himself will also be subjected to the one who put all things under him, that God may be everything to every one.

GOSPEL

R   Mark 16:1–7
L   Mark 16:1–8

¹When the sabbath was past, Mary Magdelene, and Mary the mother of James, and Salome, bought spices, so that they might go and anoint Jesus. And very early on the first day of the week they went to the tomb when the sun had risen. And they were saying to one another, "Who will roll away the stone for us from the door of the tomb?" And looking up, they saw that the stone was rolled back—it was very large. And entering the tomb, they saw a youth sitting on the right side, dressed in a white robe; and they were amazed. And the youth said to them, "Do not be amazed; you seek Jesus of Nazareth, who was crucified. He has risen, he is not here; see the place where they laid him. ⁷But go, tell his disciples and Peter that he is going before you to Galilee; there you will see him, as he told you." ⁸And they went out and fled from the tomb; for trembling and astonishment had come upon them; and they said nothing to any one, for they were afraid.

E   Matthew 28:1–10

¹Now after the sabbath, toward the dawn of the first day of the week, Mary Magdelene and the other Mary went to see the sepulchre. And behold, there was a great earthquake; for an angel of the Lord descended from heaven and came and rolled back the stone, and sat upon it. The appearance of the angel was like lightning, and its raiment white as snow. And for fear of the angel the guards trembled and became as if dead. But the angel said to the women, "Do not be afraid; for I know that you seek Jesus who was crucified. He is not here; for he has risen, as he said. Come, see the place where he lay. Then go quickly and tell his disciples that he has risen from the dead, and behold, he is going before you to Galilee; there you will see him. Lo, I have told you." So they departed quickly from

the tomb with fear and great joy, and ran to tell his disciples. And behold, Jesus met them and said, "Hail!" And they came up and took hold of Jesus' feet and worshiped him. [10]Then Jesus said to them, "Do not be afraid; go and tell my brothers to go to Galilee, and there they will see me."

R E **EASTER DAY**
L **THE RESURRECTION OF OUR LORD**

FIRST READING

R Acts 10:34a, 37–43

E Acts 10:34–43

[34a]Peter opened his mouth and said: [34b]"Truly I perceive that God shows no partiality, but in every nation any one who is God-fearing and does what is right is acceptable to God. You know the word which God sent to Israel, preaching good news of peace by Jesus Christ (who is Lord of all), [37]the word which was proclaimed throughout all Judea, beginning from Galilee after the baptism which John preached: how God anointed Jesus of Nazareth with the Holy Spirit and with power; how Jesus went about doing good and healing all that were oppressed by the devil, for God was with him. And we are witnesses to all that Jesus did both in the country of the Judeans and in Jerusalem. They put him to death by hanging him on a tree; but God raised Jesus on the third day and made him manifest; not to all the people but to us who were chosen by God as witnesses, who ate and drank with Jesus after he rose from the dead. And Jesus commanded us to preach to the people; and to testify that he is the one ordained by God to be judge of the living and the dead. [43]To this Jesus all the prophets bear witness that every one who believes in him receives forgiveness of sins through his name."

L Isaiah 25:6–9

[6]On this mountain the LORD of hosts will make for all peoples a feast of fat things, a feast of wine on the lees, of fat things full of marrow, of wine on the lees well refined. And the LORD will destroy on this mountain the covering that is cast over all peoples, the veil that is spread over all nations. The LORD will swallow up death for ever, and the Lord GOD will wipe away tears from all faces, and the reproach of God's people the LORD will take away from all the earth; for the LORD has spoken.

⁹It will be said on that day, "Lo, this is our God, for whom we have waited, that God might save us. This is the LORD, for whom we have waited; let us be glad and rejoice in the salvation of the LORD."

SECOND READING

R E Colossians 3:1–4

¹If then you have been raised with Christ, seek the things that are above, where Christ is, seated at the right hand of God. Set your minds on things that are above, not on things that are on earth. For you have died, and your life is hid with Christ in God. ⁴When Christ who is our life appears, then you also will appear with him in glory.

L 1 Corinthians 15:19–28

¹⁹If for this life only we have hoped in Christ, we are of all humankind most to be pitied.

But in fact Christ has been raised from the dead, the first fruits of those who have fallen asleep. For as by a human being came death, by a human being has come also the resurrection of the dead. For as in Adam all die, so also in Christ shall all be made alive. But each in the corresponding order: Christ the first fruits, then at his coming those who belong to Christ. Then comes the end, when Christ delivers the dominion to God, the Father, after destroying every rule and every authority and power. For Christ must reign until he has put all his enemies under his feet. The last enemy to be destroyed is death. "For God has put all things in subjection under the feet of him." But when it says, "All things are put in subjection under him," it is plain that the one is excepted who put all things under him. ²⁸When all things are subjected to Christ, then the Son himself will also be subjected to the one who put all things under him, that God may be everything to every one.

GOSPEL

R John 20:1–9

¹Now on the first day of the week Mary Magdalene came to the tomb early, while it was still dark, and saw that the stone had been taken away from the tomb. So she ran, and went to Simon Peter and the other disciple, the one whom Jesus loved, and said to them, "They have taken the Lord out of the tomb, and we do not know where they have laid him." Peter then came out with the other disciple, and they went toward the tomb. They both ran, but the other disciple outran Peter and reached the tomb first; and stooping to look in, he saw the linen cloths lying there, but did not go in. Then Simon Peter came, following him, and went into the tomb; he saw the linen cloths lying, and the napkin, which had been on Jesus' head, not lying with the linen cloths but rolled up in a place by itself. Then the other disciple, who reached the tomb first, also went in, and he saw and believed; ⁹for as yet they did not know the scripture, that Jesus must rise from the dead.

E L Mark 16:1–8

¹When the sabbath was past, Mary Magdelene, and Mary the mother of James, and Salome, bought spices, so that they might go and anoint Jesus. And very early on the first day of the week they went to the tomb when the sun had risen. And they were saying to one another, "Who will roll away the stone for us from the door of the tomb?" And looking up, they saw that the stone was rolled back—it was very large. And entering the tomb, they saw a youth sitting on the right side, dressed in a white robe; and they were amazed. And the youth said to them, "Do not be amazed; you seek Jesus of Nazareth, who was crucified. He has risen, he is not here; see the place where they laid him. But go, tell his disciples and Peter that he is going before you to Galilee; there you will see him, as he told you." ⁸And they went out and fled from the tomb; for trembling and astonishment had come upon them; and they said nothing to any one, for they were afraid.

FIRST READING

R Acts 4:32–35

³²Now the company of those who believed were of one heart and soul, and they all said that the things which they possessed were not their own, but they had everything in common. And with great power the apostles gave their testimony to the resurrection of the Lord Jesus, and great grace was upon them all. There was not a needy person among them, for as many as were possessors of lands or houses sold them, and brought the proceeds of what was sold ³⁵and laid it at the apostles' feet; and distribution was made to each as any had need.

E Acts 3:12a, 13–15, 17–26
L Acts 3:13–15, 17–26

^{12a}When Peter saw the people, he addressed them, ¹³"The God of Abraham and of Isaac and of Jacob, the God of our forebears, glorified Jesus, the servant of God, whom you delivered up and denied in the presence of Pilate, when Pilate had decided to release him. But you denied the Holy and Righteous One, and asked for a murderer to be granted to you, ¹⁵and killed the Author of life, whom God raised from the dead. To this we are witnesses.

¹⁷"And now, my dear people, I know that you acted in ignorance, as did also your rulers. But what God foretold by the mouth of all the prophets, that the Christ of God should suffer, was thus fulfilled. Repent therefore, and turn again, that your sins may be blotted out, that times of refreshing may come from the presence of the Lord, and that God may send the Christ appointed for you, Jesus, whom heaven must receive until the time for establishing all that God spoke by the mouth of the holy prophets from of old. Moses said, 'The Lord God will raise up for you a prophet from your kin as God raised me up. You shall listen to the prophet in whatever he tells you. And it shall be that every soul that does not listen to that prophet shall be destroyed from the people.' And all the prophets who have spoken, from Samuel and those who came afterwards,

also proclaimed these days. You are the children of the prophets and of the covenant which God gave to your forebears, saying to Abraham, 'And in your posterity shall all the families of the earth be blessed.' 26Having raised up the servant of God, in order to bless you in turning everyone of you from your wickedness, God sent him first to you."

SECOND READING

R E L   1 John 5:1–6

1Every one who believes that Jesus is the Christ is a child of God, and every one who loves the parent loves the child. By this we know that we love the children of God, when we love God and obey God's commandments. For this is the love of God, that we keep God's commandments, which are not burdensome. For whatever is born of God overcomes the world; and this is the victory that overcomes the world, our faith. Who is it that overcomes the world but any one who believes that Jesus is the Son of God?

6This is the one who came by water and blood, Jesus Christ, not with the water only but with the water and the blood.

GOSPEL

R E L   John 20:19–31

19On the evening of that day, the first day of the week, the doors being shut where the disciples were, for fear of the Judeans, Jesus came and stood among them and said to them, "Peace be with you." Having said this, Jesus showed them his hands and his side. Then the disciples were glad when they saw the Lord. Jesus said to them again, "Peace be with you. As the Father has sent me, even so I send you." Having said this, Jesus breathed on them, and said to them, "Receive the Holy Spirit. If you forgive the sins of any, they are forgiven; if you retain the sins of any, they are retained."

Now Thomas, one of the twelve, called the Twin, was not with them when Jesus came. So the other disciples told Thomas, "We have seen the Lord." But he said to them, "Unless I see in his hands the print of the nails, and place my finger in the mark of the nails, and place my hand in his side, I will not believe."

Eight days later, Jesus' disciples were again in the house, and Thomas was with them. The doors were shut, but Jesus came and stood among them, and said, "Peace be with you." Then Jesus said to Thomas, "Put your finger here, and see my hands; and put out your hand, and place it in my side; do not be faithless, but believing." Thomas answered Jesus, "My Lord and my God!" Jesus said to him, "Have you believed because you have seen me? Blessed are those who have not seen and yet believe."

Now Jesus did many other signs in the presence of the disciples, which are not written in this book; [31]but these are written that you may believe that Jesus is the Christ, the Son of God, and that believing you may have life in his name.

FIRST READING

R   Acts 3:13–15, 17–19

[Peter said to the people,]

¹³"The God of Abraham and of Isaac and of Jacob, the God of our forebears, glorified Jesus, the servant of God, whom you delivered up and denied in the presence of Pilate, when Pilate had decided to release him. But you denied the Holy and Righteous One, and asked for a murderer to be granted to you, ¹⁵and killed the Author of life, whom God raised from the dead. To this we are witnesses.

¹⁷"And now, my dear people, I know that you acted in ignorance, as did also your rulers. But what God foretold by the mouth of all the prophets, that the Christ of God should suffer, was thus fulfilled. ¹⁹Repent therefore, and turn again, that your sins may be blotted out, that times of refreshing may come from the presence of the Lord."

E   Acts 4:5–12
L   Acts 4:8–12

⁵On the morrow the rulers and elders and scribes were gathered together in Jerusalem, with Annas the high priest and Caiaphas and John and Alexander, and all who were of the high-priestly family. And when they had set Peter and John in the midst, they inquired, "By what power or by what name did you do this?" ⁸Then Peter, filled with the Holy Spirit, said to them, "Rulers of the people and elders, if we are being examined today concerning a good deed done to a crippled man, by what means this man has been healed, be it known to you all, and to all the people of Israel, that by the name of Jesus Christ of Nazareth, whom you crucified, whom God raised from the dead, by Jesus Christ this man is standing before you well. This is the stone which was rejected by you builders, but which has become the head of the corner. ¹²And there is salvation in no one else, for there is no other name under heaven given among humankind by which we must be saved."

SECOND READING

R   1 John 2:1–5a
E L   1 John 1:1–2:2

¹That which was from the beginning, which we have heard, which we have seen with our eyes, which we have looked upon and touched with our hands, concerning the word of life—the life was made manifest, and we saw it, and testify to it, and proclaim to you the eternal life which was with the Father and was made manifest to us—that which we have seen and heard we proclaim also to you, so that you may have communion with us; and our communion is with the Father and with Jesus Christ, the Son. And we are writing this that our joy may be complete.

This is the message we have heard from Jesus Christ and proclaim to you, that God is light and in God is no darkness at all. If we say we have communion with God while we walk in darkness, we lie and do not live according to the truth; but if we walk in the light, as God is in the light, we have communion with one another, and the blood of Jesus, God's Son, cleanses us from all sin. If we say we have no sin, we deceive ourselves, and the truth is not in us. If we confess our sins, God is faithful and just, and will forgive our sins and cleanse us from all unrighteousness. If we say we have not sinned, we make God a liar, and God's word is not in us.

¹My little children, I am writing this to you so that you may not sin; but if any one does sin, we have an advocate with the Father, Jesus Christ the righteous, ²who is the expiation for our sins, and not for ours only but also for the sins of the whole world. ³And by this we may be sure that we know God, if we keep God's commandments. They who say "I know God" but disobey God's commandments are liars, and the truth is not in them; ⁵ᵃbut those who keep God's word, in them truly love for God is perfected.

GOSPEL

R Luke 24:35–48
E Luke 24:36b–48
L Luke 24:36–49

[35]The two disciples told what had happened on the road, and how Jesus was known to them in the breaking of the bread.

[36a]As they were saying this, [36b]Jesus himself stood among them. But they were startled and frightened, and supposed that they saw a spirit. And Jesus said to them, "Why are you troubled, and why do questionings rise in your hearts? See my hands and my feet, that it is I myself; handle me, and see; for a spirit has not flesh and bones as you see that I have." And while they still disbelieved for joy, and wondered, Jesus said to them, "Have you anything here to eat?" They gave him a piece of broiled fish, and he took it and ate before them.

Then Jesus said to them, "These are my words which I spoke to you, while I was still with you, that everything written about me in the law of Moses and the prophets and the psalms must be fulfilled." Then Jesus opened their minds to understand the scriptures, and said to them, "Thus it is written, that the Christ should suffer and on the third day rise from the dead, and that repentance and forgiveness of sins should be preached in the name of Christ to all nations, beginning from Jerusalem. [48]You are witnesses of these things. [49]And behold, I send the promise of my Father upon you; but stay in the city, until you are clothed with power from on high."

FIRST READING

R Acts 4:8–12

⁸Peter, filled with the Holy Spirit, said to them, "Rulers of the people and elders, if we are being examined today concerning a good deed done to a crippled man, by what means this man has been healed, be it known to you all, and to all the people of Israel, that by the name of Jesus Christ of Nazareth, whom you crucified, whom God raised from the dead, by Jesus Christ this man is standing before you well. This is the stone which was rejected by you builders, but which has become the head of the corner. ¹²And there is salvation in no one else, for there is no other name under heaven given among humankind by which we must be saved."

E Acts 4:32–37
L Acts 4:23–33

²³When Peter and John were released they went to their friends and reported what the chief priests and the elders had said to them. And when they heard it, they lifted their voices together to God and said, "Sovereign Lord, who made the heaven and the earth and the sea and everything in them, who by the mouth of our forebear David, your servant, said by the Holy Spirit,

'Why did the Gentiles rage,
and the peoples imagine vain things?
The monarchs of the earth set themselves in array,
and the rulers were gathered together,
against the Lord and against the Lord's Anointed'—

for truly in this city there were gathered together against your holy servant Jesus, whom you anointed, both Herod and Pontius Pilate, with the Gentiles and the peoples of Israel, to do whatever your hand and your plan had predestined to take place. And now, Lord, look upon their threats, and grant to your servants to speak your word with all boldness, while you stretch out your hand to heal, and signs and wonders are performed through the name of your holy servant Jesus." And when they had prayed, the place in which they were gathered together was shaken; and they were all filled with the Holy Spirit and spoke the word of God with boldness.

[32]Now the company of those who believed were of one heart and soul, and they all said that the things which they possessed were not their own, but they had everything in common. [33]And with great power the apostles gave their testimony to the resurrection of the Lord Jesus, and great grace was upon them all. [34]There was not a needy person among them, for as many as were possessors of lands or houses sold them, and brought the proceeds of what was sold and laid it at the apostles' feet; and distribution was made to each as any had need. Thus Joseph who was surnamed by the apostles Barnabas (which means, Son of encouragement), a Levite, a native of Cyprus, [37]sold a field which belonged to him, and brought the money and laid it at the apostles' feet.

SECOND READING

R L 1 John 3:1–2
E   1 John 3:1–8

[1]See what love the Father has given us, that we should be called children of God; and so we are. The reason why the world does not know us is that it did not know God. [2]Beloved, we are God's children now; it does not yet appear what we shall be, but we know that when it appears we shall be like God, for we shall see God as God is. [3]And all who thus hope in God purify themselves as the Son is pure.

All who commit sin are guilty of lawlessness; sin is lawlessness. You know that Christ appeared to take away sins, and in him there is no sin. No one who abides in the Son sins; no one who sins has either seen or known the Son. Little children, let no one deceive you. They who do right are righteous, as Christ is righteous. [8]They who commit sin are of the devil; for the devil has sinned from the beginning. The reason the Son of God appeared was to destroy the works of the devil.

GOSPEL

R L   John 10:11–18
E   John 10:11–16

[At that time Jesus said,]

[11]"I am the good shepherd, the good shepherd who lays down his life for the sheep. The one who is a hireling and not a shepherd, whose own the sheep are not, sees the wolf coming and leaves the sheep and flees; and the wolf snatches them and scatters them. The hireling flees, caring nothing for the sheep. I am the good shepherd; I know my own and my own know me, as the Father knows me and I know the Father; and I lay down my life for the sheep. [16]And I have other sheep, that are not of this fold; I must bring them also, and they will heed my voice. So there shall be one flock, one shepherd. [17]For this reason the Father loves me, because I lay down my life, that I may take it again. [18]No one takes it from me, but I lay it down of my own accord. I have power to lay it down, and I have power to take it again; this charge I have received from my Father."

FIRST READING

R Acts 9:26–31

[26]When Saul had come to Jerusalem, he attempted to join the disciples; and they were all afraid of him, for they did not believe that he was a disciple. But Barnabas took him, and brought him to the apostles, and declared to them how on the road Saul had seen the Lord, who spoke to him, and how at Damascus he had preached boldly in the name of Jesus. So Saul went in and out among them at Jerusalem, preaching boldly in the name of the Lord. And he spoke and disputed against the Hellenists; but they were seeking to kill him. And when the community knew it, they brought him down to Caesarea, and sent him off to Tarsus.

[31]So the church thoughout all Judea and Galilee and Samaria had peace and was built up; and walking in the fear of the Lord and in the comfort of the Holy Spirit it was multiplied.

E L Acts 8:26–40

[26]An angel of the Lord said to Philip, "Rise and go toward the south to the road that goes down from Jerusalem to Gaza." This is a desert road. And Philip rose and went. And behold, an Ethiopian, a eunuch, a minister of the Candace, queen of the Ethiopians, in charge of all her treasure, had come to Jerusalem to worship and was returning; seated in his chariot, he was reading the prophet Isaiah. And the Spirit said to Philip, "Go up and join this chariot." So Philip ran to him, and heard him reading Isaiah the prophet, and asked, "Do you understand what you are reading?" And he said, "How can I, unless some one guides me?" And he invited Philip to come up and sit with him. Now the passage of the scripture which he was reading was this:

"As a sheep led to the slaughter
or a lamb before its shearer is dumb,
so he opens not his mouth.
In his humiliation justice was denied him.

Who can describe his origin?
For his life is taken up from the earth."

And the eunuch said to Philip, "About whom, pray, does the prophet say this, about himself or about some one else?" Then Philip opened his mouth, and beginning with this scripture he told him the good news of Jesus. And as they went along the road they came to some water, and the eunuch said, "See, here is water! What is to prevent my being baptized?" And he commanded the chariot to stop, and they both went down into the water, Philip and the eunuch, and Philip baptized him. And when they came up out of the water, the Spirit of the Lord caught up Philip; and the eunuch saw him no more, and went on his way rejoicing. ⁴⁰But Philip was found at Azotus, and passing on he preached the gospel to all the towns till he came to Caesarea.

SECOND READING

R E L   1 John 3:18–24

¹⁸Little children, let us not love in word or speech but in deed and in truth.

By this we shall know that we are of the truth, and reassure our hearts before God whenever our hearts condemn us; for God is greater than our hearts and knows everything. Beloved, if our hearts do not condemn us, we have confidence before God; and we receive from God whatever we ask, because we keep the commandments and do what is God-pleasing. And this is God's commandment, that we should believe in the name of Jesus Christ, the Son of God, and love one another, just as Jesus has commanded us. ²⁴All who keep God's commandments abide in God, and God in them. And by this we know that God abides in us, by the Spirit which God has given us.

GOSPEL

R L   John 15:1–8

[At that time Jesus said,]

1"I am the true vine, and my Father is the vinedresser. Every branch of mine that bears no fruit, my Father takes away, and every branch that does bear fruit my Father prunes, that it may bear more fruit. You are already made clean by the word which I have spoken to you. Abide in me, and I in you. As the branch cannot bear fruit by itself, unless it abides in the vine, neither can you, unless you abide in me. I am the vine, you are the branches. They who abide in me, and I in them, it is they that bear much fruit, for apart from me you can do nothing. Those who do not abide in me are cast forth as branches and wither; and the branches are gathered, thrown into the fire and burned. If you abide in me, and my words abide in you, ask whatever you will, and it shall be done for you. 8By this my Father is glorified, that you bear much fruit and so prove to be my disciples."

E   John 14:15–21

[At that time Jesus said,]

15"If you love me, you will keep my commandments. And I will pray the Father who will give you another Counselor, to be with you for ever, even the Spirit of truth, whom the world cannot receive, because it neither sees nor knows that Spirit; you know that Spirit, for that Spirit dwells in you, and will be in you.

"I will not leave you desolate; I will come to you. Yet a little while, and the world will see me no more, but you will see me; because I live, you will live also. In that day you will know that I am in my Father, and you in me, and I in you. 21They who have my commandments and keep them are those who love me; and those who love me will be loved by my Father, and I will love them and manifest myself to them."

FIRST READING

R Acts 10:25–26, 34–35, 44–48

25When Peter entered, Cornelius met him and fell down at his feet and worshiped him. 26But Peter lifted him up, saying, "Stand up; I too am a human being."

34And Peter opened his mouth and said: "Truly I perceive that God shows no partiality, 35but in every nation any one who is God-fearing and does what is right is acceptable to God."

44While Peter was still saying this, the Holy Spirit fell on all who heard the word. And the believers from among the Jewish people who came with Peter were amazed, because the gift of the Holy Spirit had been poured out even on the Gentiles. For they heard them speaking in tongues and extolling God. Then Peter declared, "Can any one forbid water for baptizing these people who have received the Holy Spirit just as we have?" 48And Peter commanded them to be baptized in the name of Jesus Christ. And they asked him to remain for some days.

E L Acts 11:19–30

19Those who were scattered because of the persecution that arose over Stephen traveled as far as Phoenicia and Cyprus and Antioch, speaking the word to none except Jews. But there were some of them, men of Cyprus and Cyrene, who on coming to Antioch spoke to the Greeks also, preaching the Lord Jesus. And the hand of the Lord was with them, and a great number that believed turned to the Lord. News of this came to the ears of the church in Jerusalem, and they sent Barnabas to Antioch. And coming and seeing the grace of God, Barnabas was glad and exhorted them all to remain faithful to the Lord with steadfast purpose; for he was a good man, full of the Holy Spirit and of faith. And a large company was added to the Lord. So Barnabas went to Tarsus to look for Saul; and finding him, Barnabas brought him to Antioch. For a whole year they met with the church, and taught a large company of people;

and in Antioch the disciples were for the first time called Christians.

Now in these days prophets came down from Jerusalem to Antioch. And one of them named Agabus stood up and foretold by the Spirit that there would be a great famine over all the world; and this took place in the days of Claudius. And the disciples determined, all according to their ability, to send relief to the community living in Judea; [30]and they did so, sending it to the elders by the hand of Barnabas and Saul.

SECOND READING

R 1 John 4:7–10
E 1 John 4:7–21
L 1 John 4:1–11

[1]Beloved, do not believe every spirit, but test the spirits to see whether they are of God; for many false prophets have gone out into the world. By this you know the Spirit of God: every spirit which confesses that Jesus Christ has come in the flesh is of God, and every spirit which does not confess Jesus is not of God. This is the spirit of antichrist, of which you heard that it was coming, and now it is in the world already. Little children, you are of God, and have overcome them; for the one who is in you is greater than the one who is in the world. They are of the world, therefore what they say is of the world, and the world listens to them. We are of God. Whoever knows God listens to us, and whoever is not of God does not listen to us. By this we know the spirit of truth and the spirit of error.

[7]Beloved, let us love one another; for love is of God, and everyone who loves is born of God and knows God. One who does not love does not know God; for God is love. In this the love of God was made manifest among us, that God sent into the world God's only Son, so that we might live through him. [10]In this is love, not that we loved God but that God loved us and sent the Son to be the expiation for our sins. [11]Beloved, if God so loved us, we also ought to love one another. [12]No one has ever seen God; if we love one another, God abides in us and God's love is perfected in us.

By this we know that we abide in God and God in us, because we have been given of God's own Spirit. And we have seen and testify that the Father has sent the Son as the Savior of the world. Those who confess that Jesus is the Son of God, God abides in them, and they in God. So we know and believe the love God has for us. God is love, and they who abide in love abide in God, and God abides in them. In this is love perfected with us, that we may have confidence for the day of judgment, because as the Son is, so are we in this world. There is no fear in love, but perfect love casts out fear. For fear has to do with punishment, and whoever fears is not perfected in love. We love, because God first loved us. Those who say, "I love God," and hate their brother or sister are liars; for they who do not love their brother or sister whom they have seen, cannot love God whom they have not seen. ²¹And this commandment we have from God, that they who love God should love their brother and sister as well.

GOSPEL

R E L John 15:9–17

[At that time Jesus said,]

⁹"As the Father has loved me, so have I loved you; abide in my love. If you keep my commandments, you will abide in my love, just as I have kept my Father's commandments and abide in my Father's love. These things I have spoken to you, that my joy may be in you, and that your joy may be full.

"This is my commandment, that you love one another as I have loved you. Greater love has no one than this, that a man lay down his life for his friends. You are my friends if you do what I command you. No longer do I call you slaves, for slaves do not know what their master is doing; but I have called you friends, for all that I have heard from my Father I have made known to you. You did not choose me, but I chose you and appointed you that you should go and bear fruit and that your fruit should abide; so that whatever you ask the Father in my name, the Father may give it to you. ¹⁷This I command you, to love one another."

R E L ASCENSION DAY

FIRST READING

R E L Acts 1:1–11

¹In the first book, O Theophilus, I have dealt with all that Jesus began to do and teach, until the day when he was taken up, having given commandment through the Holy Spirit to the apostles whom he had chosen. To them Jesus presented himself alive after his passion by many proofs, appearing to them during forty days, and speaking of the dominion of God. And while staying with them Jesus charged them not to depart from Jerusalem, but to wait for the promise of the Father, which, he said, "you heard from me, for John baptized with water, but before many days you shall be baptized with the Holy Spirit."

So when they had come together, they asked Jesus, "Lord, will you at this time restore dominion to Israel?" Jesus said to them, "It is not for you to know times or seasons which the Father has fixed by divine authority. But you shall receive power when the Holy Spirit has come upon you; and you shall be my witnesses in Jerusalem and in all Judea and Samaria and to the end of the earth." And when he had said this, as they were looking on, Jesus was lifted up, and a cloud took him out of their sight. And while they were gazing into heaven as he went, behold, two men stood by them in white robes, ¹¹and said, "O Galileans, why do you stand looking into heaven? This Jesus, who was taken up from you into heaven, will come in the same way as you saw him go into heaven."

SECOND READING

R Ephesians 1:17–23
E Ephesians 1:15–23
L Ephesians 1:16–23

¹⁵Because I have heard of your faith in the Lord Jesus and your love toward all the saints, ¹⁶I do not cease to give thanks for you, remembering you in my prayers, ¹⁷that the God of our Lord Jesus Christ, the Father of glory, may give you a spirit of wisdom and of revelation, that you may know God, having the

eyes of your hearts enlightened, that you may know what is the hope to which God has called you, what are the riches of God's glorious inheritance in the saints, and what is the immeasurable greatness of God's power in us who believe, according to the working of God's great might which was accomplished in Christ when God raised Christ from the dead and made him sit at the right hand of power in the heavenly places, far above all rule and authority and power and dominion, and above every name that is named, not only in this age but also in that which is to come; and God has put all things under the feet of Christ and has made him the head over all things for the church, ²³which is the body of Christ, the fullness of the one who fills all in all.

GOSPEL

R   Mark 16:15–20

¹⁵Jesus said to the eleven, "Go into all the world and preach the gospel to the whole creation. Whoever believes and is baptized will be saved; but whoever does not believe will be condemned. And these signs will accompany those who believe: in my name they will cast out demons; they will speak in new tongues; they will pick up serpents, and if they drink any deadly thing, it will not hurt them; they will lay their hands on the sick, and the sick will recover."

So then the Lord Jesus, having spoken to them, was taken up into heaven, and sat down at the right hand of God. ²⁰And they went forth and preached everywhere, while the Lord worked with them and confirmed the message by the signs that attended it. Amen.

E   Luke 24:49–53
L   Luke 24:44–53

⁴⁴Jesus said to the disciples, "These are my words which I spoke to you, while I was still with you, that everything written about me in the law of Moses and the prophets and the psalms must be fulfilled." Then Jesus opened their minds to understand the scriptures, and said to them, "Thus it is written, that the Christ should suffer and on the third day rise from

the dead, and that repentance and forgiveness of sins should be preached in the name of Christ to all nations, beginning from Jerusalem. You are witnesses of these things. [49]And behold, I send the promise of my Father upon you; but stay in the city, until you are clothed with power from on high."

Then Jesus led them out as far as Bethany, and lifting up his hands he blessed them. While blessing them, he parted from them, and was carried up into heaven. And they returned to Jerusalem with great joy, [53]and were continually in the temple blessing God.

R Acts 1:15–17, 20a, 20c–26
E L Acts 1:15–26

[15]In those days Peter stood up within the community (the company of people was in all about a hundred and twenty), and said, "My dear people, the scripture had to be fulfilled, which the Holy Spirit spoke beforehand by the mouth of David, concerning Judas who was guide to those who arrested Jesus. [17]For Judas was numbered among us, and was allotted his share in this ministry. [18](Now this man bought a field with the reward of his wickedness; and falling headlong he burst open in the middle and all his bowels gushed out. And it became known to all the inhabitants of Jerusalem, so that the field was called in their language Akeldama, that is, Field of Blood.) [20a]For it is written in the book of Psalms,

[20b]'Let his habitation become desolate,
and let there be no one to live in it';

and

[20c]'His office let another take.'

So one of the men who have accompanied us during all the time that the Lord Jesus went in and out among us, beginning from the baptism of John until the day when Jesus was taken up from us—one of these companions must become with us a witness to his resurrection." And they put forward two, Joseph called Barsabbas, who was surnamed Justus, and Matthias. And they prayed and said, "Lord, who knows the hearts of all, show which one of these two you have chosen to take the place in this ministry and apostleship from which Judas turned aside, to go to his own place." [26]And they cast lots for them, and the lot fell on Matthias; and he was enrolled with the eleven apostles.

SECOND READING

R 1 John 4:11–16

L 1 John 4:13–21

¹¹Beloved, if God so loved us, we also ought to love one another. No one has ever seen God; if we love one another, God abides in us and God's love is perfected in us.

¹³By this we know that we abide in God and God in us, because we have been given of God's own Spirit. And we have seen and testify that the Father has sent the Son as the Savior of the world. Those who confess that Jesus is the Son of God, God abides in them, and they in God. ¹⁶So we know and believe the love God has for us. God is love, and they who abide in love abide in God, and God abides in them. ¹⁷In this is love perfected with us, that we may have confidence for the day of judgment, because as the Son is, so are we in this world. There is no fear in love, but perfect love casts out fear. For fear has to do with punishment, and whoever fears is not perfected in love. We love, because God first loved us. Those who say, "I love God," and hate their brother or sister are liars; for they who do not love their brother or sister whom they have seen, cannot love God whom they have not seen. ²¹And this commandment we have from God, that they who love God should love their brother and sister as well.

E 1 John 5:9–15

⁹If we receive human testimony, the testimony of God is greater; for this is the testimony of God, that God has borne witness to the Son. They who believe in the Son of God have the testimony in themselves. They who do not believe God have made God a liar, because they have not believed in the testimony that God has borne to the Son of God. And this is the testimony, that God gave us eternal life, and this life is in the Son of God. Whoever has the Son has life; whoever has not the Son of God has not life.

I write this to you who believe in the name of the Son of God, that you may know that you have eternal life. And this is the confidence which we have in God, that if we ask anything according to God's will, God hears us. [15]And if we know that we are heard in whatever we ask, we know that we have obtained the requests made of God.

GOSPEL

John 17:11b–19

[At that time Jesus said,]

[11b]"Holy Father, keep in your name the ones whom you have given me, that they may be one, even as we are one. While I was with them, I kept them in your name, which you have given me; I have guarded them, and none of them is lost but the son of perdition, that the scripture might be fulfilled. But now I am coming to you; and these things I speak in the world, that they may have my joy fulfilled in themselves. I have given them your word; and the world has hated them because they are not of the world, even as I am not of the world. I do not pray that you should take them out of the world, but that you should keep them from the evil one. They are not of the world, even as I am not of the world. Sanctify them in the truth; your word is truth. As you sent me into the world, so I have sent them into the world. [19]And for their sake I consecrate myself, that they also may be consecrated in truth."

R PENTECOST SUNDAY
E L DAY OF PENTECOST

FIRST READING

R E Acts 2:1–11

¹When the day of Pentecost had come, the company was all together in one place. And suddenly a sound came from heaven like the rush of a mighty wind, and it filled all the house where they were sitting. And there appeared to them tongues as of fire, distributed and resting on each one of them. And they were all filled with the Holy Spirit and began to speak in other tongues, as the Spirit gave them utterance.

Now there were dwelling in Jerusalem Jewish people, devout people from every nation under heaven. And at this sound the multitude came together, and they were bewildered, because all heard them speaking in their own language. And they were amazed and wondered, saying, "Are not all these who are speaking Galileans? And how is it that we hear, all of us in our own native language? Parthians and Medes and Elamites and residents of Mesopotamia, Judea and Cappadocia, Pontus and Asia, Phrygia and Pamphylia, Egypt and the parts of Libya belonging to Cyrene, and visitors from Rome, both Jewish born and proselytes, ¹¹Cretans and Arabians, we hear them telling in our own tongues the mighty works of God."

L Ezekiel 37:1–14

¹The hand of the LORD was upon me, and brought me out by the Spirit of the LORD, and set me down in the midst of the valley; it was full of bones. And the LORD led me round among them; and behold, there were very many upon the valley; and lo, they were very dry. And the LORD said to me, "O human one, can these bones live?" And I answered, "O Lord GOD, you know." Again the LORD said to me, "Prophesy to these bones, and say to them, O dry bones, hear the word of the LORD. Thus says the Lord GOD to these bones: Behold, I will cause breath to enter you, and you shall live. And I will lay sinews upon you, and will cause flesh to come upon you, and cover

you with skin, and put breath in you, and you shall live; and you shall know that I am the LORD."

So I prophesied as I was commanded; and as I prophesied, there was a noise, and behold, a rattling; and the bones came together, bone to its bone. And as I looked, there were sinews on them, and flesh had come upon them, and skin had covered them; but there was no breath in them. Then the LORD said to me, "Prophesy to the breath, prophesy, O human one, and say to the breath, Thus says the Lord GOD: Come from the four winds, O breath, and breathe upon these slain, that they may live." So I prophesied as the LORD commanded me, and the breath came into them, and they lived, and stood upon their feet, an exceedingly great host.

Then the LORD said to me, "O human one, these bones are the whole house of Israel. Behold, they say, 'Our bones are dried up, and our hope is lost; we are clean cut off.' Therefore prophesy, and say to them, Thus says the Lord GOD: Behold, I will open your graves, and raise you from your graves, O my people; and I will bring you home into the land of Israel. And you shall know that I am the LORD, when I open your graves, and raise you from your graves, O my people. ¹⁴And I will put my Spirit within you, and you shall live, and I will place you in your own land; then you shall know that I, the LORD, have spoken, and I have done it, says the LORD."

SECOND READING

R 1 Corinthians 12:3b–7, 12–13
E 1 Corinthians 12:4–13

³ᵇNo one can say "Jesus is Lord" except by the Holy Spirit.

⁴Now there are varieties of gifts, but the same Spirit; and there are varieties of service, but the same Lord; and there are varieties of working, but it is the same God who inspires them all in every one. ⁷To each is given the manifestation of the Spirit for the common good. ⁸To one is given through the Spirit the utterance of wisdom, and to another the utterance of knowledge according to the same Spirit, to another faith by the same

Spirit, to another gifts of healing by the one Spirit, to another the working of miracles, to another prophesy, to another the ability to distinguish between spirits, to another various kinds of tongues, to another the interpretation of tongues. All these are inspired by one and the same Spirit, who chooses what to apportion to each one individually.

¹²For just as the body is one and has many parts, and all the parts of the body, though many, are one body, so it is with Christ. ¹³For by one Spirit we were all baptized into one body—Jews or Greeks, slaves or free—and all were made to drink of one Spirit.

L Acts 2:1-21

¹When the day of Pentecost had come, the company was all together in one place. And suddenly a sound came from heaven like the rush of a mighty wind, and it filled all the house where they were sitting. And there appeared to them tongues as of fire, distributed and resting on each one of them. And they were all filled with the Holy Spirit and began to speak in other tongues, as the Spirit gave them utterance.

Now there were dwelling in Jerusalem Jewish people, devout people from every nation under heaven. And at this sound the multitude came together, and they were bewildered, because all heard them speaking in their own language. And they were amazed and wondered, saying, "Are not all these who are speaking Galileans? And how is it that we hear, all of us in our own native language? Parthians and Medes and Elamites and residents of Mesopotamia, Judea and Cappadocia, Pontus and Asia, Phrygia and Pamphylia, Egypt and the parts of Libya belonging to Cyrene, and visitors from Rome, both Jewish born and proselytes, Cretans and Arabians, we hear them telling in our own tongues the mighty works of God." And all were amazed and perplexed, saying to one another, "What does this mean?" But others mocking said, "They are filled with new wine."

But Peter, standing with the eleven, lifted up his voice and addressed them, "O you Jewish people and all who dwell in Jerusalem, let this be known to you, and give ear to my words. For these people are not drunk, as you suppose, since it is only the third hour of the day; but this is what was spoken by the prophet Joel:

'And in the last days it shall be, God declares,
that I will pour out my Spirit upon all flesh,
and your sons and your daughters shall prophesy,
and your youths shall see visions,
and your elders shall dream dreams;
yes, and on my menservants and my maidservants in those
    days
I will pour out my Spirit; and they shall prophesy.
And I will show wonders in the heaven above
and signs on the earth beneath,
blood, and fire, and vapor of smoke;
the sun shall be turned into darkness
and the moon into blood,
before the day of the Lord comes,
the great and manifest day.
^{21}And it shall be that whoever calls on the name of the Lord
    shall be saved.' "

GOSPEL

R E   John 20:19–23

^{19}On the evening of that day, the first day of the week, the doors being shut where the disciples were, for fear of the Judeans, Jesus came and stood among them and said to them, "Peace be with you." Having said this, Jesus showed them his hands and his side. Then the disciples were glad when they saw the Lord. Jesus said to them again, "Peace be with you. As the Father has sent me, even so I send you." Having said this, Jesus breathed on them, and said to them, "Receive the Holy Spirit. ^{23}If you forgive the sins of any, they are forgiven; if you retain the sins of any, they are retained."

L John 7:37–39a

³⁷On the last day of the feast, the great day, Jesus stood up and proclaimed, "Let those who thirst come to me. Let those who believe in me drink. As the scripture has said, 'Out of his heart shall flow rivers of living water.' " ³⁹ᵃNow this Jesus said about the Spirit, which those who believed in him were to receive.

FIRST READING

R Deuteronomy 4:32–34, 39–40

[Moses said to the people,]

³²"Ask now of the days that are past, which were before you, since the day that God created humankind upon the earth, and ask from one end of heaven to the other, whether such a great thing as this has ever happened or was ever heard of. Did any people ever hear the voice of a god speaking out of the midst of the fire, as you have heard, and still live? ³⁴Or has any god ever attempted to go and claim a nation from the midst of another nation, by trials, by signs, by wonders, and by war, by a mighty hand and an outstretched arm, and by great terrors, according to all that the LORD your God did for you in Egypt before your eyes? ³⁹Know therefore this day, and lay it to your heart, that the LORD is God in heaven above and on the earth beneath; there is no other. ⁴⁰Therefore you shall keep the statutes and the commandments of the LORD, which I command you this day, that it may go well with you, and with your children after you, and that you may prolong your days in the land which the LORD your God gives you for ever."

E Exodus 3:1–16

¹Moses was keeping the flock of his father-in-law, Jethro, the priest of Midian; and he led his flock to the west side of the wilderness, and came to Horeb, the mountain of God. And the angel of the LORD appeared to Moses in a flame of fire out of the midst of a bush; and he looked, and lo, the bush was burning, yet it was not consumed. And Moses said, "I will turn aside and see this great sight, why the bush is not burnt." When the LORD saw that he turned aside to see, God called to him out of the bush, "Moses, Moses!" And he said, "Here am I." Then God said, "Do not come near; put off your shoes from your feet, for the place on which you are standing is holy ground." And God said, "I am the God of your father, the God of Abraham, the God of Isaac, and the God of Jacob." And Moses hid his face, for he was afraid to look at God.

Then the LORD said, "I have seen the affliction of my people who are in Egypt, and have heard their cry because of their overseers; I know their sufferings, and I have come down to deliver them out of the hand of the Egyptians, and to bring them up out of that land to a good and broad land, a land flowing with milk and honey, to the place of the Canaanites, the Hittites, the Amorites, the Perizzites, the Hivites, and the Jebusites. And now, behold, the cry of the people of Israel has come to me, and I have seen the oppression with which the Egyptians oppress them. Come, I will send you to Pharaoh that you may bring forth my people, the children of Israel, out of Egypt." But Moses said to God, "Who am I that I should go to Pharaoh, and bring the children of Israel out of Egypt?" God said, "But I will be with you; and this shall be the sign for you, that I have sent you: when you have brought forth the people out of Egypt, you shall serve God upon this mountain."

Then Moses said to God, "If I come to the people of Israel and say to them, 'The God of your forebears has sent me to you,' and they ask me, 'What is this god's name?' what shall I say to them?" God said to Moses, "I AM WHO I AM." And God said, "Say this to the people of Israel, 'I AM has sent me to you.' " God also said to Moses, "Say this to the people of Israel, 'The LORD, the God of your forebears, the God of Abraham, the God of Isaac, and the God of Jacob, has sent me to you': this is my name for ever, and thus I am to be remembered throughout all generations. [16]Go and gather the elders of Israel together, and say to them, 'The LORD, the God of your forebears, the God of Abraham, of Isaac, and of Jacob, has appeared to me, saying, "I have observed you and what has been done to you in Egypt." ' "

L   Deuteronomy 6:4–9

[Moses said to the people,]

[4]"Hear, O Israel: The LORD our God is one LORD; and you shall love the LORD your God with all your heart, and with all your soul, and with all your might. And these words which I command you this day shall be upon your heart; and you shall teach them diligently to your children, and shall talk of them

when you sit in your house, and when you walk by the way, and when you lie down, and when you rise. And you shall bind them as a sign upon your hand, and they shall be as frontlets between your eyes. ⁹And you shall write them on the doorposts of your house and on your gates."

SECOND READING

R L Romans 8:14–17
E Romans 8:12–17

¹²My dear people, we are debtors, not to the flesh, to live according to the flesh—for if you live according to the flesh you will die, but if by the Spirit you put to death the deeds of the body you will live. ¹⁴For all who are led by the Spirit of God are children of God. For you did not receive the spirit of slavery to fall back into fear, but you have received the spirit of adoption. When we cry, "Abba! Father!" it is that very Spirit bearing witness with our spirit that we are children of God, ¹⁷and if children, then heirs, heirs of God and joint heirs with Christ, provided we suffer with Christ in order that we may also be glorified with Christ.

GOSPEL

R Matthew 28:16–20

¹⁶Now the eleven disciples went to Galilee, to the mountain to which Jesus had directed them. And when they saw Jesus they worshiped him; but some doubted. And Jesus came and said to them, "All authority in heaven and on earth has been given to me. Go therefore and make disciples of all nations, baptizing them in the name of the Father and of the Son and of the Holy Spirit, ²⁰teaching them to observe all that I have commanded you; and lo, I am with you always, to the close of the age."

E John 3:1–16
L John 3:1–17

¹Now there was one of the Pharisees, named Nicodemus, a ruler of the Jewish people. He came to Jesus by night and said to him, "Rabbi, we know that you are a teacher come from God; for no one can do these signs that you do, except with the

presence of God." Jesus said to Nicodemus, "Truly, truly, I say to you, unless one is born anew, one cannot see the dominion of God." Nicodemus said to Jesus, "How can a person be born when that person is old? Can one enter a second time into the womb and be born?" Jesus answered, "Truly, truly, I say to you, unless one is born of water and the Spirit, one cannot enter the dominion of God. That which is born of the flesh is flesh, and that which is born of the Spirit is spirit. Do not marvel that I said to you, 'You must be born anew.' The wind blows where it wills, and you hear the sound of it, but you do not know whence it comes or whither it goes; so it is with every one who is born of the Spirit." Nicodemus said to Jesus, "How can this be?" Jesus answered him, "Are you a teacher of Israel, and yet you do not understand this? Truly, truly, I say to you, we speak of what we know, and bear witness to what we have seen; but you do not receive our testimony. If I have told you earthly things and you do not believe, how can you believe if I tell you heavenly things? No one has ascended into heaven but the one who descended from heaven, the Man of Heaven. And as Moses lifted up the serpent in the wilderness, so must the Man of Heaven be lifted up, that whoever believes in that one may have eternal life."

[16]For God loved the world in this way, that God gave the Son, the only begotten one, that whoever believes in him should not perish but have eternal life. [17]For God sent the Son into the world, not to condemn the world, but that through the Son the world might be saved.

R THE BODY AND BLOOD OF CHRIST

FIRST READING

R Exodus 24:3–8

³Moses came and told the people all the words of the LORD and all the ordinances; and all the people answered with one voice, and said, "All the words which the LORD has spoken we will do." And Moses wrote all the words of the LORD. And he rose early in the morning, and built an altar at the foot of the mountain, and twelve pillars, according to the twelve tribes of Israel. And Moses sent youths of the people of Israel, who offered burnt offerings and sacrificed peace offerings of oxen to the LORD. And Moses took half of the blood and put it in basins, and half of the blood he threw against the altar. Then he took the book of the covenant, and read it in the hearing of the people; and they said, "All that the LORD has spoken we will do, and we will be obedient." ⁸And Moses took the blood and threw it upon the people, and said, "Behold the blood of the covenant which the LORD has made with you in accordance with all these words."

SECOND READING

R Hebrews 9:11–15

¹¹When Christ appeared as a high priest of the good things that have come, then through the greater and more perfect tent (not made with hands, that is, not of this creation) he entered once for all into the Holy Place, taking not the blood of goats and calves but his own blood, thus securing an eternal redemption. For if the sprinkling of defiled persons with the blood of goats and bulls and with the ashes of a heifer sanctifies for the purification of the flesh, how much more shall the blood of Christ, who through the eternal Spirit offered himself without blemish to God, purify your conscience from dead works to serve the living God.

¹⁵Therefore Christ is the mediator of a new covenant, so that those who are called may receive the promised eternal inheri-

tance, since a death has occurred which redeems them from the transgressions under the first covenant.

GOSPEL

R Mark 14:12–16, 22–26

[12]On the first day of Unleavened Bread, when they sacrified the passover lamb, Jesus' disciples said to him, "Where will you have us go and prepare for you to eat the passover?" And Jesus sent two of his disciples, and said to them, "Go into the city, and someone carrying a jar of water will meet you; follow him, and wherever he enters, say to the householder, 'The Teacher says, Where is my guest room, where I am to eat the passover with my disciples?' The householder will show you a large upper room furnished and ready; there prepare for us." [16]And the disciples set out and went to the city, and found it as Jesus had told them; and they prepared the passover.

[22]And as they were eating, Jesus took bread, and blessed, and broke it, and gave it to them, and said, "Take; this is my body." And he took a cup, and having given thanks he gave it to them, and they all drank of it. And he said to them, "This is my blood of the covenant, which is poured out for many. Truly, I say to you, I shall not drink again of the fruit of the vine until that day when I drink it new in the dominion of God."

[26]And when they had sung a hymn, they went out to the Mount of Olives.

FIRST READING

R L Deuteronomy 5:12–15
E Deuteronomy 5:6–21

⁶"I am the LORD your God, who brought you out of the land of Egypt, out of the house of bondage.

"You shall have no other gods before me.

"You shall not make for yourself a graven image, or any likeness of any thing that is in heaven above, or that is on earth beneath, or that is in the water under the earth; you shall not bow down to them or serve them; for I the LORD your God am a jealous God, visiting the iniquity of the parents upon the children to the third and fourth generation of those who hate me, but showing steadfast love to thousands of those who love me and keep my commandments.

"You shall not take the name of the LORD your God in vain: for the LORD will not hold guiltless one who takes in vain the divine name.

¹²"Observe the sabbath day, to keep it holy, as the LORD your God commanded you. Six days you shall labor, and do all your work; but the seventh day is a sabbath to the LORD your God; in it you shall not do any work, you, or your son, or your daughter, or your manservant, or your maidservant, or your ox, or your donkey, or any of your cattle, or the sojourner who is within your gates, that your manservant and your maidservant may rest as well as you. ¹⁵You shall remember that you were a servant in the land of Egypt, and the LORD your God brought you out thence with a mighty hand and an outstretched arm; therefore the LORD your God commanded you to keep the sabbath day.

¹⁶"Honor your father and your mother, as the LORD your God commanded you; that your days may be prolonged, and that it

may go well with you, in the land which the LORD your God gives you.

"You shall not kill.

"Neither shall you commit adultery.

"Neither shall you steal.

"Neither shall you bear false witness against your neighbor.

²¹"Neither shall you covet your neighbor's wife; and you shall not desire your neighbor's house, or field, or manservant, or maidservant, or ox, or donkey, or anything that is your neighbor's."

SECOND READING

R 2 Corinthians 4:6–11
E L 2 Corinthians 4:5–12

⁵What we preach is not ourselves, but Jesus Christ as Lord, with ourselves as your servants for Jesus' sake. ⁶For it is the God who said, "Let light shine out of darkness," who has shone in our hearts to give the light of the knowledge of the glory of God in the face of Christ.

But we have this treasure in earthern vessels, to show that the transcendent power belongs to God and not to us. We are afflicted in every way, but not crushed; perplexed, but not driven to despair; persecuted, but not forsaken; struck down, but not destroyed; always carrying in the body the death of Jesus, so that the life of Jesus may also be manifested in our bodies. ¹¹For while we live we are always being given up to death for Jesus' sake, so that the life of Jesus may be manifested in our mortal flesh. ¹²So death is at work in us, but life in you.

GOSPEL

R E L Mark 2:23–28

²³One sabbath Jesus was going through the grainfields; and as they made their way his disciples began to pluck heads of grain. And the Pharisees said to him, "Look, why are they do-

ing what is not lawful on the sabbath?" And Jesus said to them, "Have you never read what David did, when in need and hungry, he and those who were with him: how he entered the house of God, when Abiathar was high priest, and ate the bread of the Presence, which it is not lawful for any but the priests to eat, and also gave it to those who were with him?" And Jesus said to them, "The sabbath was made for humankind, not humankind for the sabbath; [28]so the Man of Heaven is lord even of the sabbath."

R TENTH SUNDAY IN ORDINARY TIME
E PROPER 5
L THIRD SUNDAY AFTER PENTECOST

FIRST READING

R L Genesis 3:9–15
   E Genesis 3:8–21

⁸The man and the woman heard the sound of the Lᴏʀᴅ God walking in the garden in the cool of the day, and they hid themselves from the presence of the Lᴏʀᴅ God among the trees of the garden. ⁹But the Lᴏʀᴅ God called to the man, and said to him, "Where are you?" And he said, "I heard the sound of you in the garden, and I was afraid, because I was naked; and I hid myself." God said, "Who told you that you were naked? Have you eaten of the tree of which I commanded you not to eat?" The man said, "The woman whom you gave to be with me, she gave me fruit of the tree, and I ate." Then the Lᴏʀᴅ God said to the woman, "What is this that you have done?" The woman said, "The serpent beguiled me, and I ate." The Lᴏʀᴅ God said to the serpent,

"Because you have done this,
    cursed are you above all cattle,
    and above all wild animals;
upon your belly you shall go,
    and dust you shall eat
    all the days of your life.
¹⁵I will put enmity between you and the woman,
    and between your offspring and her offspring;
her offspring shall bruise your head,
    and you shall bruise his heel."
¹⁶To the woman God said,
    "I will greatly multiply your pain in childbearing;
    in pain you shall bring forth children,
yet your desire shall be for your husband,
    and he shall rule over you."

And to Adam God said,

"Because you have listened to the voice of your wife,
    and have eaten of the tree
of which I commanded you,
    'You shall not eat of it,'
cursed is the ground because of you;
    in toil you shall eat of it all the days of your life;
thorns and thistles it shall bring forth to you;
    and you shall eat the plants of the field.
In the sweat of your face
    you shall eat bread
till you return to the ground,
    for out of it you were taken;
you are dust,
    and to dust you shall return."

The man called his wife's name Eve, because she was the mother of all living. ²¹And the Lord God made for Adam and for his wife garments of skins, and clothed them.

SECOND READING

R   2 Corinthians 4:13–5:1
E L 2 Corinthians 4:13–18

¹³Since we have the same spirit of faith as was written, "I believed, and so I spoke," we too believe, and so we speak, knowing that the one who raised the Lord Jesus will raise us also with Jesus and present us together with you. For it is all for your sake, so that as grace extends to more and more people it may increase thanksgiving, to the glory of God.

So we do not lose heart. Though our outer nature is wasting away, our inner nature is being renewed every day. For this slight momentary affliction is preparing for us an eternal weight of glory beyond all comparison, ¹⁸because we look not to the things that are seen but to the things that are unseen; for the things that are seen are transient, but the things that are unseen are eternal.

¹For we know that if the earthly tent we live in is destroyed, we have a building from God, a house not made with hands, eternal in the heavens.

GOSPEL

R E L Mark 3:20–35

²⁰The crowd came together again, so that Jesus and the disciples could not even eat. And when his family heard it, they went out to seize him, for people were saying, "He is beside himself." And the scribes who came down from Jerusalem said, "He is possessed by Beelzebul, and casts out the demons by the prince of demons." And Jesus called them to him, and said to them in parables, "How can Satan cast out Satan? If a dominion is divided against itself, that dominion cannot stand. And if a house is divided against itself, that house will not be able to stand. And if Satan has risen up against Satan and is divided, Satan cannot stand, but is coming to an end. But no one can enter a strong man's house and plunder his goods without first binding the strong man; then indeed the house can be plundered.

"Truly, I say to you, all sins will be forgiven human beings, and whatever blasphemies they utter; but whoever blasphemes against the Holy Spirit never has forgiveness, but is guilty of an eternal sin"—for they had said, "He has an unclean spirit."

And the mother and the brothers of Jesus came; and standing outside they sent to him and called him. And a crowd was sitting about him; and they said to him, "Your mother and your brothers are outside, asking for you." And Jesus replied, "Who are my mother and my brothers?" And looking around on those who sat about him, Jesus said, "Here are my mother and my brothers! ³⁵Whoever does the will of God is my brother, and sister, and mother."

FIRST READING

R L Ezekiel 17:22–24

²²Thus says the Lord GOD: "I myself will take a sprig from the lofty top of the cedar, and will set it out; I will break off from the topmost of its young twigs a tender one, and I myself will plant it upon a high and lofty mountain; on the mountain height of Israel will I plant it, that it may bring forth boughs and bear fruit, and become a noble cedar; and under it will dwell all kinds of beasts; in the shade of its branches birds of every sort will nest. ²⁴And all the trees of the field shall know that I the LORD bring low the high tree, and make high the low tree, dry up the green tree, and make the dry tree flourish. I the LORD have spoken, and I will do it."

E Ezekiel 31:1–6, 10–14

¹In the eleventh year, in the third month, on the first day of the month, the word of the LORD came to me: "O human one, say to Pharaoh king of Egypt and to his multitude:

"Whom are you like in your greatness?
Behold, I will liken you to a cedar in Lebanon,
with fair branches and forest shade,
    and of great height,
    its top among the clouds.
The waters nourished it,
    the deep made it grow tall,
making its rivers flow
    round the place of its planting,
sending forth its streams
    to all the trees of the forest.
So it towered high
    above all the trees of the forest;
its boughs grew large
    and its branches long,

from abundant water in its shoots.
[6]All the birds of the air
    made their nests in its boughs;
under its branches all the beasts of the field
    brought forth their young;
and under its shadow
    dwelt all great nations.

[10]"Therefore thus says the Lord GOD: Because it towered high and set its top among the clouds, and its heart was proud of its height, I will give it into the hand of a mighty one of the nations, who shall surely deal with it as its wickedness deserves. I have cast it out. Foreigners, the most terrible of the nations, will cut it down and leave it. On the mountains and in all the valleys its branches will fall, and its boughs will lie broken in all the watercourses of the land; and all the peoples of the earth will go from its shadow and leave it. Upon its ruin will dwell all the birds of the air, and upon its branches will be all the beasts of the field. [14]All this is in order that no trees by the waters may grow to lofty height or set their tops among the clouds, and that no trees that drink water may reach up to them in height; for they are all given over to death, to the nether world among human mortals, with those who go down to the Pit."

SECOND READING

R   2 Corinthians 5:6–10
E L 2 Corinthians 5:1–10

[1]We know that if the earthly tent we live in is destroyed, we have a building from God, a house not made with hands, eternal in the heavens. Here indeed we groan, and long to put on our heavenly dwelling, so that by putting it on we may not be found naked. For while we are still in this tent, we sigh with anxiety; not that we would be unclothed, but that we would be further clothed, so that what is mortal may be swallowed up by life. The one who has prepared us for this very thing is God, who has given us the Spirit as a guarantee.

[6]So we are always of good courage; we know that while we are at home in the body we are away from the Lord, for we walk by faith, not by sight. We are of good courage, and we would rather be away from the body and at home with the Lord. So whether we are at home or away, we make it our aim to please the Lord. [10]For we must all appear before the judgment seat of Christ, so that each one may receive good or evil, according to what was done in the body.

GOSPEL

R E L   Mark 4:26–34

[26]Jesus said, "The dominion of God is as if someone should scatter seed upon the ground, and should sleep and rise night and day, and the seed should sprout and grow, the sower knows not how. The earth produces of itself, first the blade, then the ear, then the full grain in the ear. But when the grain is ripe, at once the sower puts in the sickle, because the harvest has come."

And Jesus said, "With what can we compare the dominion of God, or what parable shall we use for it? It is like a grain of mustard seed, which, when sown upon the ground, is the smallest of all the seeds on earth; yet when it is sown it grows up and becomes the greatest of all shrubs, and puts forth large branches, so that the birds of the air can make nests in its shade."

With many such parables Jesus spoke the word to them, as they were able to hear it; [34]he did not speak to them without a parable, but privately to his own disciples Jesus explained everything.

R TWELFTH SUNDAY IN ORDINARY TIME
E PROPER 7
L FIFTH SUNDAY AFTER PENTECOST

FIRST READING

R Job 38:1, 8–11
E Job 38:1–11, 16–18
L Job 38:1–11

¹The LORD answered Job out of the whirlwind:
²"Who is this that darkens counsel
   by words without knowledge?
Arm yourself like a warrior,
   I will question you, and you shall declare to me.
Where were you when I laid the foundation of the earth?
   Tell me, if you have understanding.
Who determined its measurements—surely you know!
   Or who stretched the line upon it?
On what were its bases sunk,
   or who laid its cornerstone,
when the morning stars sang together,
   and all the heavenly beings shouted for joy?
⁸Or who shut in the sea with doors,
   when it burst forth from the womb;
when I made clouds its garment,
   and thick darkness its swaddling band,
and prescribed bounds for it,
   and set bars and doors,
¹¹and said, 'Thus far shall you come, and no farther,
   and here shall your proud waves be stayed'?
¹⁶Have you entered into the springs of the sea,
   or walked in the recesses of the deep?
Have the gates of death been revealed to you,
   or have you seen the gates of deep darkness?
¹⁸Have you comprehended the expanse of the earth?
   Declare, if you know all this."

SECOND READING

R 2 Corinthians 5:14–17
E L 2 Corinthians 5:14–21

¹⁴The love of Christ controls us, because we are convinced that one has died for all; therefore all have died. And he died for all, that those who live might live no longer for themselves but for the one who for their sake died and was raised.

From now on, therefore, we regard no one from a human point of view; even though we once regarded Christ from a human point of view, we regard him thus no longer. ¹⁷Therefore, anyone being in Christ is a new creation; the old has passed away, behold, the new has come. ¹⁸All this is from God. By God through Christ, we have been reconciled to God, who gave us the message of reconciliation; that is, God was in Christ, reconciling the world to God, not counting their trespasses against them, and entrusting to us the message of reconciliation. So we are ambassadors for Christ, God appealing through us. We beseech you on behalf of Christ, be reconciled to God. ²¹For our sake God made to be sin the one who knew no sin, so that in Christ we might become the righteousness of God.

GOSPEL

R E L Mark 4:35–41

³⁵On that day, when evening had come, Jesus said to the disciples, "Let us go across to the other side." And leaving the crowd, they took him with them in the boat, just as he was. And other boats were with him. And a great storm of wind arose, and the waves beat into the boat, so that the boat was already filling. But Jesus was in the stern, asleep on the cushion; and they woke him and said to him, "Teacher, do you not care if we perish?" And Jesus awoke and rebuked the wind, and said to the sea, "Peace! Be still!" And the wind ceased, and there was a great calm. Jesus said to them, "Why are you afraid? Have you no faith?" ⁴¹And they were filled with awe, and said to one another, "Who then is this, that even wind and sea obey him?"

R TWELFTH SUNDAY IN ORDINARY TIME 175
E PROPER 7
L FIFTH SUNDAY AFTER PENTECOST

R **THIRTEENTH SUNDAY IN ORDINARY TIME**
E **PROPER 8**
L **SIXTH SUNDAY AFTER PENTECOST**

FIRST READING

R Wisdom 1:13–15, 2:23–24

¹³God did not make death,
and does not delight in the death of the living.
For God created all things that they might exist,
and the generative forces of the world are wholesome,
and there is no destructive poison in them;
and the dominion of Hades is not on earth.
¹⁵For righteousness is immortal.
²³For God created humankind for incorruption,
and made human beings in the image of God's own eternity,
²⁴but through the devil's envy death entered the world,
and those who belong to the devil's party experience it.

E Deuteronomy 15:7–11

[Moses said to the people,]

⁷"If there is among you someone who is poor, one of your kin,
in any of your towns within your land which the LORD your
God gives you, you shall not harden your heart or shut your
hand against your poor neighbor, but you shall open your
hand and lend to the poor what is sufficient to fill the need,
whatever it may be. Take heed lest there be a base thought in
your heart, and you say, 'The seventh year, the year of release
is near,' and your eye be hostile to your poor neighbor, and
you give your neighbor nothing, and your neighbor cry to the
LORD against you, and it be sin in you. You shall give to your
neighbor freely, and your heart shall not be grudging when
you give; because for this the LORD your God will bless you in
all your work and in all that you undertake. ¹¹For the poor will
never cease out of the land; therefore I command you, You
shall open wide your hand to your neighbor, to the needy and
to the poor, in the land."

L · Lamentations 3:22–33

²²The steadfast love of the LORD never ceases,
   the mercies of the LORD never come to an end;
they are new every morning;
   great is your faithfulness.
"The LORD is my portion," says my soul,
   "therefore in the LORD will I hope."
The LORD is good to those who are patient,
   to the soul that seeks after God.
It is good that one should wait quietly
   for the salvation of the LORD.
It is good for a mighty man that he bear
   the yoke during youth.
Let him sit alone in silence
   when God has laid it on him;
let him put his mouth in the dust—
   there may yet be hope;
let him give his cheek to the smiter,
   and be filled with insults.
For the Lord will not
   cast off for ever,
but, though causing grief, the Lord will have compassion,
   out of an abundance of steadfast love
²²for the LORD does not willingly afflict
   or grieve men such as this.

SECOND READING

R   2 Corinthians 8:7, 9, 13–15
E   2 Corinthians 8:1–9, 13–15
L   2 Corinthians 8:1–9, 13–14

¹We want you to know, my dear people, about the grace of
God which has been shown in the churches of Macedonia, for
in a severe test of affliction, their abundance of joy and their
extreme poverty have overflowed in a wealth of liberality on
their part. For they gave according to their means, as I can testify, and beyond their means, of their own free will, begging us
earnestly for the favor of taking part in the relief of the saints—

R   THIRTEENTH SUNDAY IN ORDINARY TIME   177
E   PROPER 8
L   SIXTH SUNDAY AFTER PENTECOST

and this, not as we expected, but first they gave themselves to the Lord and to us by the will of God. Accordingly we have urged Titus that as he had already made a beginning, he should also complete among you this gracious work. [7]Now as you excel in everything—in faith, in utterance, in knowledge, in all earnestness, and in your love for us—see that you excel in this gracious work also.

[8]I say this not as a command, but to prove by the earnestness of others that your love also is genuine. [9]For you know the grace of our Lord Jesus Christ, that though he was rich, yet for your sake he became poor, so that by his poverty you might become rich. [13]I do not mean that others should be eased and you burdened, [14]but that as a matter of equality your abundance at the present time should supply their want, so that their abundance may supply your want, that there may be equality. [15]As it is written, "One who gathered much had nothing over, and one who gathered little had no lack."

GOSPEL

R Mark 5:21–24, 35b–43
E Mark 5:22–24, 35b–43
L Mark 5:21–24a, 35–43

[21]When Jesus had crossed again in the boat to the other side, a great crowd gathered about him; and he was beside the sea. [22]Then came one of the rulers of the synagogue, Jairus by name; and seeing Jesus, he fell at his feet, and besought him, saying, "My little daughter is at the point of death. Come and lay your hands on her, so that she may be made well, and live." [24a]And Jesus went with him.

[24b]And a great crowd followed him and thronged about him.

[35a]While Jesus was still speaking, [35b]there came from the ruler's house some who said, "Your daughter is dead. Why trouble the Teacher any further?" But ignoring what they said, Jesus said to the ruler of the synagogue, "Do not fear, only believe." And Jesus allowed no one to follow him except Peter and James and John the brother of James. When they came to the house of

the ruler of the synagogue, Jesus saw a tumult, and people weeping and wailing loudly. And when he had entered, he said to them, "Why do you make a tumult and weep? The child is not dead but sleeping." And they laughed at him. But he put them all outside, and took the child's father and mother and those who were with him, and went in where the child was. Taking her by the hand Jesus said to her, "Talitha cumi"; which means, "Little girl, I say to you, arise." And immediately the girl got up and walked (she was twelve years of age), and they were immediately overcome with amazement. [43]And Jesus strictly charged them that no one should know this, and told them to give her something to eat.

FIRST READING

R Ezekiel 2:2–5
E Ezekiel 2:1–7
L Ezekiel 2:1–5

¹The LORD said to me, "O human one, stand upon your feet, and I will speak with you." ²And when the LORD spoke to me, the Spirit entered into me and set me upon my feet; and I heard the LORD speaking to me, saying, "O human one, I send you to the people of Israel, to a nation of rebels, who have rebelled against me; they and their forebears have transgressed against me to this very day. The people also are impudent and stubborn: I send you to them; and you shall say to them, 'Thus says the Lord GOD.' ⁵And whether they hear or refuse to hear (for they are a rebellious house) they will know that there has been a prophet among them. ⁶And you, O human one, be not afraid of them, nor be afraid of their words, though briers and thorns are with you and you sit upon scorpions; be not afraid of their words, nor be dismayed at their looks, for they are a rebellious house. ⁷And you shall speak my words to them, whether they hear or refuse to hear; for they are a rebellious house."

SECOND READING

R L 2 Corinthians 12:7–10
E 2 Corinthians 12:2–10

²I know someone in Christ who fourteen years ago was caught up to the third heaven—whether in the body or out of the body I do not know, God knows. And I know that this person was caught up into Paradise—whether in the body or out of the body I do not know, God knows—and heard unspeakable words which may not be uttered by human speech. On behalf of this person I will boast, but on my own behalf I will not boast, except of my weaknesses. Though if I wish to boast, I

shall not be a fool, for I shall be speaking the truth. But I refrain from it, so that people may not think more of me than they see in me or hear from me. [7]And to keep me from being too elated by the abundance of revelations, a thorn was given me in the flesh, a messenger of Satan, to harass me, to keep me from being too elated. Three times I besought the Lord about his, that it should leave me; but the Lord said to me, "My grace is sufficient for you, for my power is made perfect in weakness." I will all the more gladly boast of my weaknesses, that the power of Christ may rest upon me. [10]For the sake of Christ, then, I am content with weaknesses, insults, hardships, persecutions, and calamities; for when I am weak, then I am strong.

GOSPEL

R E L   Mark 6:1–6

[1]Jesus went away from there and came to his own country; and his disciples followed him. And on the sabbath he began to teach in the synagogue; and many who heard him were astonished, saying, "From where did these things come to him? What is the wisdom given to him? What mighty works are wrought by his hands! Is not this the carpenter, the son of Mary and brother of James and Joses and Judas and Simon, and are not his sisters here with us?" And they took offense at him. And Jesus said to them, "Prophets are not without honor, except in their own country, and among their own kin, and in their own house." And Jesus could do no mighty work there, except that he laid his hands upon a few sick people and healed them. [6]And he marveled because of their unbelief.

And he went about among the villages teaching.

FIRST READING

R Amos 7:12–15
E Amos 7:7–15
L Amos 7:10–15

⁷The Lord GOD showed me: behold, the Lord was standing beside a wall built with a plumb line, holding a plumb line. And the LORD said to me, "Amos, what do you see?" And I said, "A plumb line." Then the Lord said,

"Behold, I am setting a plumb line
    in the midst of my people Israel;
    I will never again pass by them;
the high places of Isaac shall be made desolate,
    and the sanctuaries of Israel shall be laid waste,
    and I will rise against the house of Jeroboam with the
        sword."

¹⁰Then Amaziah the priest of Bethel sent to Jeroboam king of Israel, saying, "Amos has conspired against you in the midst of the house of Israel; the land is not able to bear all his words. For thus Amos has said,

'Jeroboam shall die by the sword,
    and Israel must go into exile
    away from its land.' "

¹²And Amaziah said to Amos, "O seer, go, flee away to the land of Judah, and eat bread there, and prophesy there; but never again prophesy at Bethel, for it is the king's sanctuary, and it is a temple of the kingdom."

Then Amos answered Amaziah, "I am no prophet, nor a prophet's son; but I am a shepherd, and a dresser of sycamore trees, ¹⁵and the LORD took me from following the flock, and the LORD said to me, 'Go, prophesy to my people Israel.' "

SECOND READING

R Ephesians 1:3–10
E Ephesians 1:1–14
L Ephesians 1:3–14

[1]Paul, an apostle of Christ Jesus by the will of God,

To the saints who are also faithful in Christ Jesus:
Grace to you and peace from God, our Father, and the Lord
    Jesus Christ.

[3]Blessed be the God and Father of our Lord Jesus Christ, who
has blessed us in Christ with every spiritual blessing in the
heavenly places, even as God chose us in Christ before the
foundation of the world, that before God we should be holy
and blameless. God destined us in love for adoption through
Jesus Christ: this was God's good pleasure and will, to the
praise of God's glorious grace freely bestowed on us in the Beloved, in whom we have redemption through his blood, the
forgiveness of our trespasses, according to the riches of God's
grace lavished upon us. For God has made known to us in all
wisdom and insight the mystery of the divine will, according to
God's purpose set forth in Christ [10]as a plan for the fullness to
time, to unite all things in Christ, things in heaven and things
on earth.

[11]In Christ, according to the purpose of the one who accom-
plishes all things according to the counsel of divine will, we
who first hoped in Christ have been destined and appointed to
live for the praise of God's glory. In Christ you also, who have
heard the word of truth, the gospel of your salvation, and have
believed in him, were sealed with the promised Holy Spirit,
[14]which is the guarantee of our inheritance until we acquire
possession of it, to the praise of God's glory.

GOSPEL

Mark 6:7–13

[7]Jesus summoned the twelve, and began to send them out two by two, and gave them authority over the unclean spirits. He charged them to take nothing for their journey except a staff; no bread, no bag, no money in their belts; but to wear sandals and not put on two tunics. And Jesus said to them, "Where you enter a house, stay there until you leave the place. And if any place will not receive you and they refuse to hear you, when you leave, shake off the dust that is on your feet for a testimony against them." So they went out and preached that people should repent. [13]And they cast out many demons, and anointed with oil many that were sick and healed them.

R SIXTEENTH SUNDAY IN ORDINARY TIME
E PROPER 11
L NINTH SUNDAY AFTER PENTECOST

FIRST READING

R L Jeremiah 23:1–6

¹"Woe to the shepherds who destroy and scatter the sheep of my pasture!" says the LORD. Therefore thus says the LORD, the God of Israel, concerning the shepherds who care for my people: "You have scattered my flock, and have driven them away, and you have not attended to them. Behold, I will attend to you for your evil doings, says the LORD. Then I will gather the remnant of my flock out of all the countries where I have driven them, and I will bring them back to their fold, and they shall be fruitful and multiply. I will set shepherds over them who will care for them, and they shall fear no more, nor be dismayed, neither shall any be missing, says the LORD.

"Behold, the days are coming, says the LORD, when I will raise up for David a righteous Branch, who shall reign as king and deal wisely, and shall execute justice and righteousness in the land. ⁶In his days Judah will be saved, and Israel will dwell securely. And this is the name by which he will be called: 'The LORD is our righteousness.' "

E Isaiah 57:14b–21

¹⁴ᵇ"Build up, build up, prepare the way,
    remove every obstruction from my people's way."
For thus says the high and lofty One
    who inhabits eternity, whose name is Holy:
"I dwell in the high and holy place,
    and also with those who are of a contrite and humble spirit,
to revive the spirit of the humble,
    and to revive the heart of the contrite.
For I will not contend for ever,
    nor will I always be angry;
for from me proceeds the spirit,
    and I have made the breath of life.

Because of the iniquity of their covetousness I was angry
  I smote them, I hid my face and was angry;
    but they went on backsliding in the way of their own heart.
I have seen their ways, but I will heal them;
  I will lead them and requite them with comfort,
    creating for their mourners the fruit of the lips.
Peace, peace, to the far and to the near; says the LORD;
  and I will heal them.
But the wicked are like the tossing sea;
  for it cannot rest,
    and its waters toss up mire and dirt.
²¹There is no peace, says my God, for the wicked."

SECOND READING

R   Ephesians 2:13–18
E   Ephesians 2:11–22
L   Ephesians 2:13–22

¹¹Remember that at one time you Gentiles in the flesh, called the uncircumcision by what is called the circumcision, which is made in the flesh by hands—remember that you were at that time separated from Christ, alienated from the commonwealth of Israel, and strangers to the covenants of promise, having no hope and without God in the world. ¹³But now in Christ Jesus you who once were far off have been brought near in the blood of Christ. For Christ is our peace, who had made us both one, and has broken down the dividing wall of hostility, by abolishing in his flesh the law of commandments and ordinances, in order to create in himself one new human being in place of the two, so making peace, and might reconcile us both to God in one body through the cross, thereby bringing the hostility to an end. And he came and preached peace to you who were far off and peace to those who were near; ¹⁸for through him we both have access in one Spirit to the Father. ¹⁹So then you are no longer strangers and sojourners, but you are citizens together with the saints and members of the household of God, built upon the foundation of apostles and prophets, Christ Jesus himself being the cornerstone, in whom the whole structure is joined together and grows into a holy temple in the Lord; ²²in

186   SIXTEENTH SUNDAY IN ORDINARY TIME   R
      PROPER 11   E
      NINTH SUNDAY AFTER PENTECOST   L

whom you also are built into it for a dwelling place of God in the Spirit.

GOSPEL

R L   Mark 6:30–34
  E   Mark 6:30–44

[30]The apostles returned to Jesus, and told him all that they had done and taught. And he said to them, "Come away by yourselves to a lonely place, and rest a while." For many were coming and going, and they had no leisure even to eat. And they went away in the boat to a lonely place by themselves. Now many saw them going, and knew them, and they ran there on foot from all the towns, and got there ahead of them. [34]Going ashore, Jesus saw a great throng, and had compassion on them, because they were like sheep without a shepherd; and he began to teach them many things. [35]And when it grew late, his disciples came to him and said, "This is a lonely place, and the hour is now late; send them away, to go into the country and villages round about and buy themselves something to eat." But Jesus answered them, "You give them something to eat." And they said to him, "Shall we go and buy two hundred denarii worth of bread, and give it to them to eat?" And Jesus said to them, "How many loaves have you? Go and see." And when they had found out, they said, "Five, and two fish." Then Jesus commanded them all to sit down by companies upon the green grass. So they sat down in groups, by hundreds and by fifties. And taking the five loaves and the two fish he looked up to heaven, and blessed, and broke the loaves, and gave them to the disciples to set before the people; and he divided the two fish among them all. And they all ate and were satisfied. And they took up twelve baskets full of broken pieces and of the fish. [44]And those who ate the loaves were five thousand men.

R SEVENTEENTH SUNDAY IN ORDINARY TIME
E PROPER 12
L TENTH SUNDAY AFTER PENTECOST

FIRST READING

R 2 Kings 4:42–44

⁴²A certain man came from Baal-shalishah, bringing Elisha, the man of God, bread of the first fruits, twenty loaves of barley, and fresh ears of grain in his sack. And Elisha said, "Give to the people, that they may eat." But his servant said, "How am I to set this before a hundred men?" So Elisha repeated, "Give them to the people, that they may eat, for thus says the LORD, 'They shall eat and have some left.' " ⁴⁴So he set it before them. And they ate, and had some left, according to the word of the LORD.

E 2 Kings 2:1–15

¹When the LORD was about to take Elijah up to heaven by a whirlwind, Elijah and Elisha were on their way from Gilgal. And Elijah said to Elisha, "Tarry here, I pray you; for the LORD has sent me as far as Bethel." But Elisha said, "As the LORD lives, and as you yourself live, I will not leave you." So they went down to Bethel. And the prophets who were in Bethel came out to Elisha, and said to him, "Do you know that today the LORD will take away your master from over you?" And Elisha said, "Yes, I know it; hold your peace."

Elijah said to him, "Elisha, tarry here, I pray you; for the LORD has sent me to Jericho." But Elisha said, "As the LORD lives, and as you yourself live, I will not leave you." So they came to Jericho. The prophets who were at Jericho drew near to Elisha, and said to him, "Do you know that today the LORD will take away your master from over you?" And he answered, "Yes, I know it; hold your peace."

Then Elijah said to Elisha, "Tarry here, I pray you; for the LORD has sent me to the Jordan." But Elisha said, "As the LORD lives, and as you yourself live, I will not leave you." So the two of them went on. Fifty men from among the prophets also went, and stood at some distance from them, as they both were standing by the Jordan. Then Elijah took his mantle, and rolled it up, and struck the water, and the water was parted to the one side and to the other, till the two of them could go over on dry ground.

When they had crossed, Elijah said to Elisha, "Ask what I shall do for you, before I am taken from you." And Elisha said, "I pray you, let me inherit a double share of your spirit." And Elijah said, "You have asked a hard thing; yet, if you see me as I am being taken from you, it shall be so for you; but if you do not see me, it shall not be so." And as they still went on and talked, behold, a chariot of fire and horses of fire separated the two of them. And Elijah went up by a whirlwind into heaven. And Elisha saw it and cried, "My father, my father! the chariot of Israel and its riders!" And Elisha saw Elijah no more.

Then Elisha took hold of his own clothes and rent them in two pieces. And he took up the mantle of Elijah that had fallen from him, and went back and stood on the bank of the Jordan. Then he took the mantle of Elijah that had fallen from him, and struck the water, saying, "Where is the Lord, the God of Elijah?" And when he had struck the water, the water was parted to the one side and to the other; and Elisha went over.

^{15}Now when the prophets who were at Jericho saw him over against them, they said, "The spirit of Elijah rests on Elisha." And they came to meet him, and bowed to the ground before him.

L   Exodus 24:3–11

^{3}Moses came and told the people all the words of the Lord and all the ordinances; and all the people answered with one voice, and said, "All the words which the Lord has spoken we will do." And Moses wrote all the words of the Lord. And he rose early in the morning, and built an altar at the foot of the mountain, and twelve pillars, according to the twelve tribes of Israel. And Moses sent youths of the people of Israel, who offered burnt offerings and sacrificed peace offerings of oxen to the Lord. And Moses took half of the blood and put it in basins, and half of the blood he threw against the altar. Then he took the book of the covenant, and read it in the hearing of the people; and they said, "All that the LORD has spoken we will do, and we will be obedient." And Moses took the blood and threw it upon the people, and said, "Behold the blood of the covenant which the LORD has made with you in accordance with all these words."

Then Moses and Aaron, Nadab, and Abihu, and seventy of the elders of Israel went up, and they saw the God of Israel; and there was under God's feet as it were a pavement of sapphire stone, like the very heaven for clearness. [11]And the LORD did not lay a hand on the leaders of the people of Israel; they beheld God, and ate and drank.

SECOND READING

R   Ephesians 4:1–6
E L Ephesians 4:1–7, 11–16

[1]I therefore, a prisoner for the Lord, beg you to lead a life worthy of the calling to which you have been called, with all lowliness and meekness, with patience, forbearing one another in love, eager to maintain the unity of the Spirit in the bond of peace. There is one body and one Spirit, just as you were called to the one hope that belongs to your call, one Lord, one faith, one baptism, [6]one God and Father of us all, who is above all and through all and in all. [7]But grace was given to each of us according to the measure of Christ's gift.

[11]The gifts of Christ were that some should be apostles, some prophets, some evangelists, some pastors and teachers, to equip the saints for the work of ministry, for building up the body of Christ, until we all attain to the unity of the faith and of the knowledge of the Son of God, to the perfected body, to the measure of the stature of the fullness of Christ; so that we may no longer be children, tossed to and fro and carried about with every wind of doctrine, by human cunning, by human craftiness in deceitful wiles. Rather, speaking the truth in love, we are to grow up in every way into the one who is the head, into Christ, [16]from whom the whole body, joined and knit to-

gether by every joint with which it is supplied, when each part is working properly, makes bodily growth and upbuilds itself in love.

GOSPEL

R L John 6:1–15

¹Jesus went to the other side of the Sea of Galilee, which is the Sea of Tiberias. And a multitude followed him, because they saw the signs which he did on those who were diseased. Jesus went up on the mountain, and there sat down with his disciples. Now the Passover, the feast of the Jewish people, was at hand. Lifting up his eyes, then, and seeing that a multitude was coming to him, Jesus said to Philip, "How are we to buy bread, so that these people may eat?" This Jesus said to test Philip, for he himself knew what he would do. Philip answered him, "Two hundred denarii would not buy enough bread for each of them to get a little." One of Jesus' disciples, Andrew, Simon Peter's brother, said to Jesus, "There is a child here who has five barley loaves and two fish; but what are they among so many?" Jesus said, "Make the people sit down." Now there was much grass in the place; so they sat down, the men numbering about five thousand. Jesus then took the loaves, and having given thanks, he distributed them to those who were seated; so also the fish, as much as they wanted. And when they had eaten their fill, Jesus told his disciples, "Gather up the fragments left over, that nothing may be lost." So they gathered them up and filled twelve baskets with fragments from the five barley loaves, left by those who had eaten. When the people saw the sign which Jesus had done, they said, "This is indeed the prophet who is to come into the world!"

¹⁵Perceiving then that they were about to come and take him by force to make him king, Jesus withdrew again to the mountain by himself.

E Mark 6:45–52

⁴⁵Immediately Jesus made his disciples get into the boat and go before him to the other side, to Bethsaida, while he dismissed the crowd. And having taken leave of them, he went up on the

mountain to pray. And when evening came, the boat was out on the sea, and Jesus was alone on the land. And Jesus saw that they were making headway painfully, for the wind was against them. And about the fourth watch of the night he came to them, walking on the sea. He meant to pass by them, but when they saw him walking on the sea they thought it was a ghost, and cried out; for they all saw him, and were terrified. But immediately Jesus spoke to them and said, "Take heart, it is I; have no fear." And he got into the boat with them and the wind ceased. And they were utterly astounded, [52]for they did not understand about the loaves, but their hearts were hardened.

FIRST READING

R Exodus 16:2–4, 12–15
E Exodus 16:2–4, 9–15
L Exodus 16:2–15

²The whole congregation of the people of Israel murmured against Moses and Aaron in the wilderness, and said to them, "Would that we had died by the hand of the LORD in the land of Egypt, when we sat by the pots filled with meat and ate bread to the full; for you have brought us out into this wilderness to kill this whole assembly with hunger."

⁴Then the LORD said to Moses, "Behold, I will rain bread from heaven for you; and the people shall go out and gather a day's portion every day, that I may prove them, whether they will walk in my law or not. ⁵On the sixth day, when they prepare what they bring in, it will be twice as much as they gather daily." So Moses and Aaron said to all the people of Israel, "At evening you shall know that it was the LORD who brought you out of the land of Egypt, and in the morning you shall see the glory of the LORD, because your murmurings against the LORD have been heard. For what are we, that you murmur against us?" And Moses said, "When the LORD gives you in the evening meat to eat and in the morning bread to the full, because the LORD has heard your murmurings which you murmur against the LORD—what are we? Your murmurings are not against us but against the LORD."

⁹And Moses said to Aaron, "Say to the whole congregation of the people of Israel, 'Come near before the LORD who has heard your murmurings.' " And as Aaron spoke to the whole congregation of the people of Israel, they looked toward the wilderness, and behold, the glory of the LORD appeared in the cloud. And the LORD said to Moses, ¹²"I have heard the murmurings of the people of Israel; say to them, 'At twilight

you shall eat meat, and in the morning you shall be filled with bread; then you shall know that I am the Lord your God.' "

In the evening quails came up and covered the camp; and in the morning dew lay round about the camp. And when the dew had gone up, there was on the face of the wilderness a fine, flake-like thing, fine as hoarfrost on the ground. ¹⁵When the people of Israel saw it, they said to one another, "What is it?" For they did not know what it was. And Moses said to them, "It is the bread which the Lord has given you to eat."

SECOND READING

R Ephesians 4:17, 20–24
E Ephesians 4:17–25
L Ephesians 4:17–24

¹⁷This I affirm and testify in the Lord, that you must no longer live as the Gentiles do, in the futility of their minds; ¹⁸they are darkened in their understanding, alienated from the life of God because of the ignorance that is in them, due to their hardness of heart; they have become callous and have given themselves up to licentiousness, greedy to practice every kind of uncleanness. ²⁰You did not so learn Christ!—assuming that you have heard about him and were taught in him, as the truth is in Jesus. Put off your old nature which belongs to your former manner of life and is corrupt through deceitful lusts, and be renewed in the spirit of your minds, ²⁴and put on the new nature, created after the likeness of God in true rightousness and holiness.

²⁵Therefore, putting away falsehood, let all speak the truth with their neighbors, for we are part of one another.

GOSPEL

R E L John 6:24–35

²⁴When the people saw that Jesus was not there, nor his disciples, they themselves got into the boats and went to Capernaum, seeking Jesus.

When they found him on the other side of the sea, they said to him, "Rabbi, when did you come here?" Jesus answered them, "Truly, truly, I say to you, you seek me, not because you saw signs, but because you ate your fill of the loaves. Do not labor for the food which perishes, but for the food which endures to eternal life, which the Man of Heaven will give to you; for on him God, the Father, has set the seal." Then they said to him, "What must we do, to be doing the works of God?" Jesus answered them, "This is the work of God, that you believe in the one whom God has sent." So they said to him, "Then what sign do you do, that we may see, and believe you? What work do you perform? Our forebears ate the manna in the wilderness; as it is written, 'He gave them bread from heaven to eat.'" Jesus then said to them, "Truly, truly, I say to you, it was not Moses who gave you the bread from heaven; my Father gives you the true bread from heaven. For the bread of God is that which comes down from heaven, and gives life to the world." They said to him, "Lord, give us this bread always."

[35]Jesus said to them, "I am the bread of life; they who come to me shall not hunger, and they who believe in me shall never thirst."

R **NINETEENTH SUNDAY IN ORDINARY TIME**
E **PROPER 14**
L **TWELFTH SUNDAY AFTER PENTECOST**

FIRST READING

R L 1 Kings 19:4–8

⁴Elijah went a day's journey into the wilderness, and came and sat down under a broom tree; and he asked that he might die, saying, "It is enough; now, O LORD, take away my life; for I am no better than my forebears." And he lay down and slept under a broom tree; and behold, an angel touched him, and said to him, "Arise and eat." And Elijah looked, and behold, there was at his head a cake baked on hot stones and a jar of water. And he ate and drank, and lay down again. And the angel of the LORD came again a second time, and touched him, and said, "Arise and eat, else the journey will be too great for you." ⁸And Elijah arose, and ate and drank, and went in the strength of that food forty days and forty nights to Horeb the mount of God.

E Deuteronomy 8:1–10

[Moses said to the people,]

¹"All the commandment which I command you this day you shall be careful to do, that you may live and multiply, and go in and possess the land which the LORD swore to give to your forebears. And you shall remember all the way which the LORD your God has led you these forty years in the wilderness, that the LORD might humble you, testing you to know what was in your heart, whether you would keep God's commandments, or not. And the LORD humbled you and let you hunger and fed you with manna, which you did not know, nor did your forebears know; that the LORD might make you know that not by bread alone does one live, but by everything that proceeds out of the mouth of the LORD. Your clothing did not wear out upon you, and your foot did not swell, these forty years. Know then in your heart that the LORD your God disciplines you, as a man disciplines his child. So you shall keep the commandments of

the LORD your God: you shall walk in God's ways and fear the LORD. For the LORD your God is bringing you into a good land, a land of brooks of water, of fountains and springs, flowing forth in valleys and hills, a land of wheat and barley, of vines and fig trees and pomegranates, a land of olive trees and honey, a land in which you will eat bread without scarcity, in which you will lack nothing, a land whose stones are iron, and out of whose hills you can dig copper. ¹⁰And you shall eat and be full, and you shall bless the LORD your God for the good land the LORD has given you."

SECOND READING

R E L Ephesians 4:30–5:2

³⁰Do not grieve the Holy Spirit of God, in whom you were sealed for the day of redemption. Let all bitterness and wrath and anger and clamor and slander be put away from you, with all malice, and be kind to one another, tenderhearted, forgiving one another, as God in Christ forgave you.

Therefore be imitators of God, as beloved children. ²And walk in love, as Christ loved us and gave himself up for us, a fragrant offering and sacrifice to God.

GOSPEL

R L John 6:41–51
E John 6:37–51

[At that time Jesus said,]

³⁷"All that the Father gives me will come to me; and those who come to me I will not cast out. For I have come down from heaven, not to do my own will, but the will of the one who sent me; and this is the will of the one who sent me, that I should lose nothing of all that the Father has given me, but raise it up at the last day. For this is the will of my Father, that all who see the Son and believe in him should have eternal life; and I will raise them up at the last day."

⁴¹The Jewish people then murmured at him, because he said, "I am the bread which came down from heaven." They said,

"Is not this Jesus, the son of Joseph, whose father and mother we know? How does he now say, 'I have come down from heaven'?" Jesus answered them, "Do not murmur among yourselves. It is not possible for people to come to me unless the Father who sent me draws them; and I will raise them up at the last day. It is written in the prophets, 'And they shall all be taught by God.' Every one who has heard and learned from the Father comes to me. No one has seen the Father except the one who is from God; this one has seen the Father. Truly, truly, I say to you, those who believe have eternal life. I am the bread of life. Your forebears ate the manna in the wilderness, and they died. This is the bread which comes down from heaven, that one may eat of it and not die. [51]I am the living bread which came down from heaven; any one who eats of this bread will live for ever; and the bread which I shall give for the life of the world is my flesh."

R TWENTIETH SUNDAY IN ORDINARY TIME
E PROPER 15
L THIRTEENTH SUNDAY AFTER PENTECOST

FIRST READING

R E L Proverbs 9:1–6

> [1]Wisdom has built her house,
>   she has set up her seven pillars.
> She has slaughtered her beasts, she has mixed her wine,
>   she has also set her table.
> She has sent out her maids to call
>   from the highest places in the town,
> "Let the simple turn in here!"
>   To whoever is without sense she says,
> "Come, eat of my bread
>   and drink of the wine I have mixed.
> [6]Leave simpleness, and live,
>   and walk in the way of insight."

SECOND READING

R E L Ephesians 5:15–20

[15]Look carefully how you walk, not as unwise but as wise, making the most of the time, because the days are evil. Therefore do not be foolish, but understand what the will of the Lord is. And do not get drunk with wine, for that is debauchery; but be filled with the Spirit, addressing one another in psalms and hymns and spiritual songs, singing and making melody to the Lord with all your heart, [20]always and for everything giving thanks in the name of our Lord Jesus Christ to God, the Father.

GOSPEL

R L John 6:51–58
E John 6:53–59

[At that time Jesus said:]

[51]"I am the living bread which came down from heaven; any who eat of this bread will live for ever; and the bread which I shall give for the life of the world is my flesh."

The Jewish people then disputed among themselves, saying, "How can this man give us his flesh to eat?" [53]So Jesus said to them, "Truly, truly, I say to you, unless you eat the flesh of the Man of Heaven and drink his blood, you have no life in you; they who eat my flesh and drink my blood have eternal life, and I will raise them up at the last day. For my flesh is food indeed, and my blood is drink indeed. They who eat my flesh and drink my blood abide in me, and I in them. As the living Father sent me, and I live because of the Father, so they who eat me will live because of me. [58]This is the bread which came down from heaven, not such as the forebears ate and died; they who eat this bread will live for ever." [59]This Jesus said in the synagogue, as he taught at Capernaum.

FIRST READING

R Joshua 24:1–2a, 15–17, 18b
E Joshua 24:1–2a, 14–25
L Joshua 24:1–2a, 14–18

¹Joshua gathered all the tribes of Israel to Shechem, and summoned the elders, the heads, the judges, and the officers of Israel; and they presented themselves before God. ²ᵃAnd Joshua said to all the people, "Thus says the LORD, the God of Israel:

¹⁴"Now therefore fear the LORD, and serve the LORD in sincerity and in faithfulness; put away the gods which your forebears served beyond the River, and in Egypt, and serve the LORD. ¹⁵And if you be unwilling to serve the LORD, choose this day whom you will serve, whether the gods your forebears served in the region beyond the River, or the gods of the Amorites in whose land you dwell; but as for me and my house, we will serve the LORD."

Then the people answered, "Far be it from us that we should forsake the LORD, to serve other gods; ¹⁷for it is the LORD our God who brought us and our forebears up from the land of Egypt, out of the house of bondage, and who did those great signs in our sight, and preserved us in all the way that we went, and among all the peoples through whom we passed; ¹⁸ᵃand the LORD drove out before us all the peoples, the Amorites who lived in the land; ¹⁸ᵇtherefore we also will serve the LORD, for the LORD is our God."

¹⁹But Joshua said to the people, "You cannot serve the LORD; for the LORD is a holy God and a jealous God and will not forgive your transgressions or your sins. If you forsake the LORD and serve foreign gods, then the LORD will turn and do you harm, and consume you, after having done you good."

And the people said to Joshua, "No; but we will serve the LORD." Then Joshua said to the people, "You are witnesses against yourselves that you have chosen to serve the LORD." And they said, "We are witnesses." Joshua said, "Then put away the foreign gods which are among you, and incline your heart to the LORD, the God of Israel." And the people said to Joshua, "The LORD our God we will serve, and the LORD's voice we will obey." 25So Joshua made a covenant with the people that day, and made statutes and ordinances for them at Shechem.

SECOND READING

R Ephesians 5:21–32 §
E Ephesians 5:21–33 §
L Ephesians 5:21–31 §

21Be subject to one another out of reverence for Christ. Wives are subject to their husbands, as to the Lord. For the husband is the head of the wife as Christ is the head of the church, the body, and is its Savior. As the church is subject to Christ, so let wives also be subject in everything to their husbands. Husbands, love your wives, as Christ loved the church and gave himself up for it, that he might sanctify it, having cleansed it by the washing of water with the word, that he might present the church to himself in splendor, without spot or wrinkle or any such thing, that it might be holy and without blemish. Even so husbands should love their wives as their own bodies. He who loves his wife loves himself. People do not hate their own bodies, but nourish and cherish them, as Christ does the church, because we are parts of his body. 31"For this reason a man shall leave his father and mother and be joined to his wife, and the two shall become one flesh." 32This mystery is a profound one, and I am saying that it refers to Christ and the church; 33however, let each husband among you love his wife as himself, and let the wife respect her husband.

GOSPEL

John 6:60–69

⁶⁰Many of Jesus' disciples, when they heard his words, said, "This is a hard saying; who can listen to it?" But Jesus, knowing in himself that his disciples murmured at it, said to them, "Do you take offense at this? Then what if you were to see the Man of Heaven ascending where he was before? It is the spirit that gives life, the flesh is of no avail; the words that I have spoken to you are spirit and life. But there are some of you that do not believe." For Jesus knew from the first who those were that did not believe, and who it was that would betray him. And he said, "This is why I told you that people are not able to come to me unless it is granted them by the Father."

After this many of his disciples drew back and no longer went about with him. Jesus said to the twelve, "Do you also wish to go away?" Simon Peter answered him, "Lord, to whom shall we go? You have the words of eternal life; ⁶⁹and we have believed, and have come to know, that you are the Holy One of God."

R TWENTY-SECOND SUNDAY IN ORDINARY TIME
E PROPER 17
L FIFTEENTH SUNDAY AFTER PENTECOST

FIRST READING

R L Deuteronomy 4:1–2, 6–8
E Deuteronomy 4:1–9

[Moses said to the people,]

¹"And now, O Israel, give heed to the statutes and the ordinances which I teach you, and do them; that you may live, and go in and take possession of the land which the LORD, the God of your forebears, gives you. ²You shall not add to the word which I command you, nor take from it; that you may keep the commandments of the LORD your God which I command you. ³Your eyes have seen what the LORD did at Baal-peor; for the LORD your God destroyed from among you all the men who followed the Baal of Peor; but you who held fast to the LORD your God are all alive this day. Behold, I have taught you statutes and ordinances, as the LORD my God commanded me, that you should do them in the land which you are entering to take possession of it. ⁶Keep them and do them; for that will be your wisdom and your understanding in the sight of the peoples, who, when they hear all these statutes, will say, 'Surely this great nation is a wise and understanding people.' For what great nation is there that has a god so near to it as the LORD our God is to us, whenever we cry out? ⁸And what great nation is there, that has statutes and ordinances so righteous as all this law which I set before you this day?

⁹"Only take heed, and keep your soul diligently, lest you forget the things which your eyes have seen, and lest they depart from your heart all the days of your life; make them known to your children and your children's children."

SECOND READING

R James 1:17–18, 21b–22, 27

¹⁷Every good endowment and every perfect gift is from above, coming down from the Father of lights with whom there is no variation or shadow due to change. ¹⁸Out of divine will God brought us forth by the word of truth that we should be a kind of first fruits of God's creatures.

²¹ᵇReceive with meekness the implanted word, which is able to save your souls. ²²But be doers of the word, and not hearers only, deceiving yourselves. ²⁷Religion that is pure and undefiled before God and the Father is this: to visit orphans and widows in their affliction, and to keep oneself unstained from the world.

E L Ephesians 6:10–20

¹⁰Be strong in the Lord and in the strength of the Lord's might. Put on the whole armor of God, that you may be able to stand against the wiles of the devil. For we are not contending against flesh and blood, but against the principalities, against the powers, against the world rulers of this present darkness, against the spiritual hosts of wickedness in the heavenly places. Therefore take the whole armor of God, that you may be able to withstand in the evil day, and having done all, to stand. Stand therefore, having girded your waist with truth, and having put on the breastplate of righteousness, and having shod your feet with the equipment of the gospel of peace; besides all these, taking the shield of faith, with which you can quench all the flaming darts of the evil one. And take the helmet of salvation, and the sword of the Spirit, which is the word of God. Pray at all times in the Spirit, with all prayer and supplication. To that end keep alert with all perserverance, making supplication for all the saints, and also for me, that utterance may be given me in opening my mouth boldly to proclaim the mystery of the gospel, ²⁰for which I am an ambassador in chains; that I may declare it boldly, as I ought to speak.

GOSPEL

Mark 7:1–8, 14–15, 21–23

¹When the Pharisees gathered together to Jesus, with some of the scribes, who had come from Jerusalem, they saw that some of his disciples ate with hands defiled, that is, unwashed. (For the Pharisees, and all the Jewish people, do not eat unless they wash their hands, observing the tradition of the elders; and when they come from the market place, they do not eat unless they purify themselves; and there are many other traditions which they observe, the washing of cups and pots and vessels of bronze.) And the Pharisees and the scribes asked Jesus, "Why do your disciples not live according to the tradition of the elders, but eat with hands defiled?" And he said to them, "Well did Isaiah prophesy of you hyprocrites, as it is written,

'This people honors me with their lips,
but their heart is far from me;
in vain do they worship me,
teaching human precepts as doctrines.'

⁸You leave the commandment of God, and hold fast to human tradition."

¹⁴And Jesus called the people to him again, and said to them, ¹⁵"Hear me, all of you, and understand: nothing which goes into a person from the outside is defiling; but the things which come out are what defile a human being. ²¹For from within, out of the human heart, come evil thoughts, fornication, theft, murder, adultery, coveting, wickedness, deceit, licentiousness, envy, slander, pride, foolishness. ²³All these evil things come from within, and they defile a human being."

FIRST READING

R E L Isaiah 35:4–7a

⁴Say to those who are of a fearful heart,
  "Be strong, fear not!
Behold, your God
  will come with vengeance,
with the recompense of God.
  God will come and save you."
Then the eyes of the blind shall be opened,
  and the ears of the deaf unstopped;
then shall the lame leap like a hart,
  and the tongue of the dumb sing for joy.
For the waters shall break forth in the wilderness,
  and streams in the desert;
⁷ᵃthe burning sand shall become a pool,
  and the thirsty ground springs of water.

SECOND READING

R James 2:1–5

¹My dear people, show no partiality as you hold the faith of
our Lord Jesus Christ, the Lord of glory. For if a person with
gold rings and in fine clothing comes into your assembly, and a
poor person in shabby clothing also comes in, and you pay attention to the one who wears the fine clothing and say, "Have
a seat here, please," while you say to the poor person, "Stand
there," or, "Sit at my feet," have you not made distinctions
among yourselves, and become judges with evil thoughts? ⁵Listen, my beloved ones. Has not God chosen those who are poor
in the world to be rich in faith and heirs of the dominion promised to those who love God?

E   James 1:17–27
L   James 1:17–22, 26–27

[17]Every good endowment and every perfect gift is from above, coming down from the Father of lights with whom there is no variation or shadow due to change. Out of divine will God brought us forth by the word of truth that we should be a kind of first fruits of God's creatures.

Know this, my beloved ones. Let every one be quick to hear, slow to speak, slow to anger, for the anger of a man does not work the righteousness of God. Therefore put away all filthiness and rank growth of wickedness and receive with meekness the implanted word, which is able to save your souls.

[22]But be doers of the word, and not hearers only, deceiving yourselves. [23]Any one who is a hearer of the word and not a doer resembles a man who observes his natural face in a mirror; for he observes himself and goes away and at once forgets what he was like. But they who look into the perfect law, the law of liberty, and persevere, being no hearers that forget but doers that act, shall be blessed in their doing.

[26]Those who think they are religious, and do not bridle their tongue but deceive their heart, their religion is vain. [27]Religion that is pure and undefiled before God and the Father is this: to visit orphans and widows in their affliction, and to keep oneself unstained from the world.

GOSPEL

R E L   Mark 7:31–37

[31]Jesus returned from the region of Tyre, and went through Sidon to the Sea of Galilee, through the region of the Decapolis. And they brought to him someone who was deaf and had a speech impediment; and they besought Jesus to lay his hand upon him. And taking him aside from the multitude privately, Jesus put his fingers into the man's ears, and spat and touched the man's tongue; and looking up to heaven, he sighed, and said to him, "Ephphatha," that is, "Be opened." And the man's ears were opened, his tongue was released, and

208   TWENTY-THIRD SUNDAY IN ORDINARY TIME   R
     PROPER 18   E
     SIXTEENTH SUNDAY AFTER PENTECOST   L

he spoke plainly. And Jesus charged them to tell no one; but the more he charged them, the more zealously they proclaimed it. [37]And they were astonished beyond measure, saying, "He has done all things well; he even makes those who are deaf to hear and those who are dumb to speak."

R TWENTY-FOURTH SUNDAY IN ORDINARY TIME
E PROPER 19
L SEVENTEENTH SUNDAY AFTER PENTECOST

FIRST READING

R Isaiah 50:5–9a
E Isaiah 50:4–9
L Isaiah 50:4–10

⁴The Lord GOD has given me
   the tongue of those who are taught,
that I may know how to sustain with a word
   those who are weary.
Morning by morning the Lord GOD wakens,
   wakens my ear,
   to hear as those who are taught.
⁵The Lord GOD has opened my ear,
   and I was not rebellious,
   I turned not backward.
I gave my back to the smiters,
   and my cheeks to those who pulled out the beard;
I hid not my face
   from shame and spitting.
For the Lord GOD helps me;
   therefore I have not been confounded;
therefore I have set my face like a flint,
   and I know that I shall not be put to shame;
   the one who vindicates me is near.
Who will contend with me?
   Let us stand up together.
Who is my adversary?
   Let my adversary come near to me.
⁹ᵃBehold, the Lord GOD helps me;
   who will declare me guilty?
⁹ᵇBehold, all of them will wear out like a garment;
   the moth will eat them up.

¹⁰Who among you fears the LORD
    and obeys the voice of the servant of God,
the servant who walks in darkness,
    and has no light,
the servant who trusts in the name of the LORD
    and relies upon his God?

SECOND READING

R James 2:14–18
E L James 2:1–5, 8–10, 14–18

¹My dear people, show no partiality as you hold the faith of our
Lord Jesus Christ, the Lord of glory. For if a person with gold
rings and in fine clothing comes into your assembly, and a poor
person in shabby clothing also comes in, and you pay attention
to the one who wears the fine clothing and say, "Have a seat
here, please," while you say to the poor person, "Stand there,"
or, "Sit at my feet," have you not made distinctions among
yourselves, and become judges with evil thoughts? ⁵Listen, my
beloved ones. Has not God chosen those who are poor in the
world to be rich in faith and heirs of the dominion promised to
those who love God?

⁸If you really fulfill the royal law, according to the scripture,
"You shall love your neighbor as yourself," you do well. But if
you show partiality, you commit sin, and are convicted by the
law as transgressors. ¹⁰For whoever keeps the whole law but
fails in one point has become guilty of all of it.

¹⁴What does it profit, my dear people, if someone claims to
have faith but has not works? Is faith able to save? If a brother
or sister is ill-clad and in lack of daily food, and one of you
says to them, "Go in peace, be warmed and filled," without
giving them the things needed for the body, what does it
profit? So faith by itself, if it has no works, is dead.

¹⁸But some one will say, "You have faith and I have works."
Show me your faith apart from your works, and I by my works
will show you my faith.

GOSPEL

R L Mark 8:27–35

E Mark 8:27–38

²⁷Jesus went on with his disciples, to the villages of Caesarea Philippi; and on the way he asked his disciples, "Who do people say that I am?" And they told him, "John the Baptist; and others say, Elijah; and others one of the prophets." And Jesus asked them, "But who do you say that I am?" Peter answered him, "You are the Christ." And he charged them to tell no one about him.

And Jesus began to teach them that the Man of Heaven must suffer many things, and be rejected by the elders and the chief priests and the scribes, and be killed, and after three days rise again. And Jesus said this plainly. And Peter took him, and began to rebuke him. But turning and seeing his disciples, Jesus rebuked Peter, and said, "Get behind me, Satan! For you are thinking in human terms, and not in those of God."

And Jesus called to him the multitude with his disciples, and said to them, "Those who would come after me, let them deny themselves and take up their cross and follow me. ³⁵For those who would save their life will lose it; and those who lose their life for my sake and the gospel's will save it. ³⁶For what does it profit them, to gain the whole world and forfeit their life? For what can they give in return for their life? ³⁸For those who are ashamed of me and of my words in this adulterous and sinful generation, of them will the Man of Heaven also be ashamed, when he comes in the glory of his Father with the holy angels."

FIRST READING

R Wisdom 2:12, 17–20
E Wisdom 1:16–2:1, 12–22

^{16}The ungodly by their words and deeds summoned death;
considering it a friend, they pined away,
and they made a covenant with it,
because they are fit to belong to its party.
^{1}For they reasoned unsoundly, saying to themselves,
"Short and sorrowful is our life,
and there is no remedy when human life comes to an end,
and no one has been known to return from Hades.
^{12}Let us lie in wait for the righteous man,
because he is inconvenient to us and opposes our actions;
he reproaches us for sins against the law,
and accuses us of sins against our training.
^{13}He professes to have knowledge of God,
and calls himself a child of the Lord.
He became to us a reproof of our thoughts;
and the very sight of him is a burden to us,
because his manner of life is unlike that of others,
and his ways are strange.
We are considered by him as something base,
and he avoids our ways as unclean,
and calls the last end of the righteous happy,
and boasts that God is his father.
^{17}Let us see if his words are true,
and let us test what will happen at the end of his life;
for if the righteous man is God's son, God will help him,
and will deliver him from the hand of his adversaries.
Let us test him with insult and torture,
that we may find out how gentle he is,
and make trial of his forebearance.
^{20}Let us condemn the righteous man to a shameful death,

for, according to what he says, he will be protected."
²¹Thus the ungodly reasoned, but they were led astray,
for their wickedness blinded them.
²²And they did not know the secret purposes of God,
nor hope for the wages of holiness,
nor discern the prize for blameless souls.

L   Jeremiah 11:18–20

¹⁸The LORD made it known to me and I knew;
    then you showed me their evil deeds.
But I was like a gentle lamb
    led to the slaughter.
I did not know it was against me
    they devised schemes, saying,
"Let us destroy the tree with its fruit,
    let us cut him off from the land of the living,
    that his name be remembered no more."
²⁰But, O LORD of hosts, judging righteously,
    trying the heart and the mind,
let me see your vengeance upon them,
    for to you have I committed my cause.

SECOND READING

R   James 3:16–4:3
E L James 3:16–4:6

¹⁶Where jealousy and selfish ambition exist, there will be disor-
der and every vile practice. But the wisdom from above is first
pure, then peaceable, gentle, open to reason, full of mercy and
good fruits, without uncertainty or insincerity. And the harvest
of righteousness is sown in peace by those who make peace.

What causes wars, and what causes fightings among you? Is it
not your passions that are at war in your bodies? You desire
and do not have; so you kill. And you covet and cannot obtain;
so you fight and wage war. You do not have, because you
do not ask. ³You ask and do not receive, because you ask
wrongly, to spend it on your passions. ⁴Unfaithful creatures!
Do you not know that friendship with the world is enmity with
God? Therefore those who wish to be friends of the world

make themselves enemies of God. Or do you suppose it is in vain that the scripture says, "God yearns jealously over the spirit which was made to dwell in us"? [6]But God gives more grace; therefore it says, "God opposes the proud, but gives grace to the humble."

GOSPEL

R E L   Mark 9:30–37

[30]Jesus and his disciples went on from there and passed through Galilee. And he would not have any one know it; for he was teaching his disciples, saying to them, "The Man of Heaven will be delivered into human hands, and they will kill him; and when he is killed, after three days he will rise." But they did not understand the saying, and they were afraid to ask him.

And they came to Capernaum; and when he was in the house he asked them, "What were you discussing on the way?" But they were silent; for on the way they had discussed with one another who was the greatest. And Jesus sat down and called the twelve, and said to them, "Any one who would be first must be last of all and servant of all." And Jesus took a child, and put it in the midst of them; and taking the child in his arms, he said to them, [37]"Whoever receives one such child in my name receives me; and whoever receives me, receives not me but the one who sent me."

FIRST READING

R Numbers 11:25–29

E L Numbers 11:4–6, 10–16, 24–29

[4]The rabble that was among the people of Israel had a craving hunger; and the people of Israel also wept again, and said, "O that we had meat to eat! We remember the fish we ate in Egypt for nothing, the cucumbers, the melons, the leeks, the onions, and the garlic; [6]but now our strength is dried up, and there is nothing at all but this manna to look at."

[10]Moses heard the people weeping throughout their families, every man at the door of his tent; and the anger of the LORD blazed hotly, and Moses was displeased. Moses said to the LORD, "Why have you dealt ill with your servant? And why have I not found favor in your sight, that you lay the burden of all this people upon me? Did I conceive all this people? Did I bring them forth, that you should say to me, 'Carry them in your bosom, as a nurse carries the sucking child, to the land which you swore to give their forebears?' Where am I to get meat to give to all this people? For they weep before me and say, 'Give us meat, that we may eat.' I am not able to carry all this people alone, the burden is too heavy for me. If you will deal thus with me, kill me at once, if I find favor in your sight, that I may not see my wretchedness."

[16]And the LORD said to Moses, "Gather for me seventy men of the elders of Israel, whom you know to be the elders of the people and officers over them; and bring them to the tent of meeting, and let them take their stand there with you."

[24]So Moses went out and told the people the words of the LORD; and he gathered seventy men of the elders of the people, and placed them round about the tent. [25]Then the LORD came down in the cloud and spoke to Moses, and took some of the spirit that was upon him and put it upon the seventy elders;

and when the spirit rested upon them, they prophesied. But they did so no more.

Now two men remained in the camp, one named Eldad, and the other named Medad, and the spirit rested upon them; they were among those registered, but they had not gone out to the tent, and so they prophesied in the camp. And a youth ran and told Moses, "Eldad and Medad are prophesying in the camp." And Joshua the son of Nun, the minister of Moses, one of his chosen ones, said, "My lord Moses, forbid them." [29]But Moses said to him, "Are you jealous for my sake? Would that all the LORD's people were prophets, that the LORD's Spirit would be given to them all!"

SECOND READING

R James 5:1–6

[1]Come now, you rich, weep and howl for the miseries that are coming upon you. Your riches have rotted and your garments are motheaten. Your gold and silver have rusted, and their rust will be evidence against you and will eat your flesh like fire. You have laid up treasure for the last days. Behold, the wages of the laborers who mowed your fields, which you kept back by fraud, cry out; and the cries of the harvesters have reached the ears of the Lord of hosts. You have lived on the earth in luxury and in pleasure; you have fattened your hearts in a day of slaughter. [6]You have condemned, you have killed the righteous one, who does not resist you.

E L James 4:7–12

[7]Submit yourselves therefore to God. Resist the devil, and the devil will flee from you. Draw near to God, and God will draw near to you. Cleanse your hands, you sinners, and purify your hearts, you doubters. Be wretched and mourn and weep. Let your laughter be turned to mourning and your joy to dejection. Humble yourselves before the Lord, and the Lord will exalt you.

Do not defame one another, my dear people. Those who defame or judge a brother or sister, defame and judge the law.

R TWENTY-SIXTH SUNDAY IN ORDINARY TIME 217
E PROPER 21
L NINETEENTH SUNDAY AFTER PENTECOST

But if you judge the law, you are not a doer of the law but a judge. [12]There is one lawgiver and judge, the one who is able to save and to destroy. But who are you that you judge your neighbor?

GOSPEL

R E L   Mark 9:38–50

[38]John said to Jesus, "Teacher, we saw someone casting out demons in your name, whom we forbade, because he was not following us." But Jesus said, "Do not forbid him; for no one who does a mighty work in my name will be able soon after to speak evil of me. For whoever is not against us is for us. For truly, I say to you, those who give you a cup of water to drink because you bear the name of Christ, will by no means lose their reward.

"Those who cause one of these little ones who believe in me to sin, it would be better for them if a great millstone were hung round their neck and they were thrown into the sea. And if your hand causes you to sin, cut it off; it is better for you to enter life maimed than with two hands to go to hell, to the unquenchable fire. And if your foot causes you to sin, cut it off; it is better for you to enter life lame than with two feet to be thrown into hell. And if your eye causes you to sin, pluck it out; it is better for you to enter the dominion of God with one eye than with two eyes to be thrown into hell, where their worm does not die, and the fire is not quenched. For every one will be salted with fire. [50]Salt is good; but if the salt has lost its saltness, how will you season it? Have salt in yourselves, and be at peace with one another."

R TWENTY-SEVENTH SUNDAY IN ORDINARY TIME
E PROPER 22
L TWENTIETH SUNDAY AFTER PENTECOST

FIRST READING

R E L Genesis 2:18–24

[18]The LORD God said, "It is not good that the man should be alone; I will make him a companion fit for him." So out of the ground the LORD God formed every beast of the field and every bird of the air, and brought them to the man to see what he would call them; and whatever the man called every living creature, that was its name. The man gave names to all cattle, and to the birds of the air, and to every beast of the field; but for the man there was not found a companion fit for him. So the LORD God caused a deep sleep to fall upon the man, and while he slept took one of his ribs and closed up its place with flesh; and the rib which the LORD God had taken from the man, the LORD God made into a woman and brought her to the man. Then the man said,

"This at last is bone of my bones
    and flesh of my flesh;
she shall be called a woman,
    because she was taken out of a man."

[24]Therefore a man leaves his father and his mother and cleaves to his wife, and they become one flesh.

SECOND READING

R L Hebrews 2:9–11
E Hebrews 2:9–18

[9]We see Jesus, who for a little while was made lower than the angels, crowned with glory and honor because of the suffering of death, so that by the grace of God Jesus might taste death for every one.

For it was fitting that God, for whom and by whom all things exist, in bringing many children to glory, should make the pioneer of their salvation perfect through suffering. [11]For the one who sanctifies and those who are sanctified have all one origin. That is why he is not ashamed to call them brothers and sisters, [12]saying,

"I will proclaim your name to my family,
in the midst of the congregation I will praise you."

And again,

"I will put my trust in God."

And again,

"Here am I, and the children God has given me."

Since therefore the children share in flesh and blood, Jesus himself likewise partook of the same nature, that through death he might destroy the one who has the power of death, that is, the devil, and deliver all those who through fear of death were subject to lifelong bondage. For surely it is not with angels that Jesus is concerned but with the descendants of Abraham. Therefore Jesus had to be made like his human family in every respect, so that he might become a merciful and faithful high priest in the service of God, to make expiation for the sins of the people. [18]For because Jesus himself has suffered and been tempted, he is able to help those who are tempted.

GOSPEL

R   Mark 10:2–12
E   Mark 10:2–9
L   Mark 10:2–16

[2]Pharisees came up and in order to test Jesus asked, "Is it lawful for a husband to divorce his wife?" Jesus answered them, "What did Moses command you?" They said, "Moses allowed a husband to write a certificate of divorce, and to put her away." But Jesus said to them, "For your hardness of heart Moses wrote you this commandment. But from the beginning of creation, 'God made them male and female.' 'For this reason a

man shall leave his father and mother and be joined to his wife, and the two shall become one flesh.' So they are no longer two but one flesh. ⁹What therefore God has joined together, let no human being put asunder."

¹⁰And in the house the disciples asked Jesus again about this matter. And he said to them, "Whatever man divorces his wife and marries another, commits adultery against her; ¹²and if she divorces her husband and marries another, she commits adultery."

¹³And they were bringing children to him, that he might touch them, and his disciples rebuked them. But seeing it Jesus was indignant, and said to them, "Let the children come to me, do not hinder them; for to such belongs the dominion of God. Truly, I say to you, whoever does not receive the dominion of God like a child shall not enter it." ¹⁶And Jesus took them in his arms and blessed them, laying his lands upon them.

TWENTY-EIGHTH SUNDAY IN ORDINARY TIME

PROPER 23

TWENTY-FIRST SUNDAY AFTER PENTECOST

FIRST READING

R   Wisdom 7:7–11

⁷I prayed, and understanding was given me;
I called upon God, and the spirit of Wisdom came to me.
I preferred her to scepters and thrones,
and I accounted wealth as nothing in comparison with her.
Neither did I liken to her any priceless gem,
because all gold is but a little sand in her sight,
and silver will be accounted as clay before her.
I loved her more than health and beauty,
and I chose to have her rather than light,
because her radiance never ceases.
¹¹All good things came to me along with her,
and in her hands uncounted wealth.

E L   Amos 5:6–7, 10–15

⁶Seek the Lord and live,
   lest the Lord break out like fire in the house of Joseph,
   and it devour, with none to quench it for Bethel,
⁷O you who turn justice to wormwood,
   and cast down righteousness to the earth!
¹⁰They hate the one reproving in the gate,
   and they abhor the one speaking the truth.
Therefore because you trample upon the poor
   and take from them exactions of wheat,
you have built houses of hewn stone,
   but you shall not dwell in them;
you have planted pleasant vineyards,
   but you shall not drink their wine.
For I know how many are your transgressions,
   and how great are your sins—
you who afflict the righteous, who take a bribe,

and turn aside the needy in the gate.
Therefore one who is prudent will keep silent in such a time;
    for it is an evil time.
Seek good, and not evil,
    that you may live;
and so the LORD, the God of hosts, will be with you,
    as you have said.
[15]Hate evil, and love good,
    and establish justice in the gate;
it may be that the LORD, the God of hosts,
    will be gracious to the remnant of Joseph.

SECOND READING

R   Hebrews 4:12–13

[12]For the word of God is living and active, sharper than any two-edged sword, piercing to the division of soul and spirit, of joints and marrow, and discerning the thoughts and intentions of the heart. [13]And before God no creature is hidden, but all are open and laid bare to the eyes of the one with whom we have to do.

E L   Hebrews 3:1–6

[1]My dear and holy people, who share in a heavenly call, consider Jesus, the apostle and high priest of our confession. Jesus was faithful to the one who appointed him, just as Moses also was faithful in God's house. Yet Jesus has been counted worthy of as much more glory than Moses as the builder of a house has more honor than the house. (For every house is built by some one, but the builder of all things is God.) Now Moses was faithful in all God's house as a servant, to testify to the things that were to be spoken later, [6]but Christ was faithful over God's house as a son. And we are God's house if we hold fast our confidence and pride in our hope.

R   TWENTY-EIGHTH SUNDAY IN ORDINARY TIME   **223**
E   PROPER 23
L   TWENTY-FIRST SUNDAY AFTER PENTECOST

GOSPEL

R E L Mark 10:17–27

[17]As Jesus was setting out on his journey, a man ran up and knelt before him, and asked him, "Good Teacher, what must I do to inherit eternal life?" And Jesus said to him, "Why do you call me good? No one is good but God alone. You know the commandments: 'Do not kill, Do not commit adultery, Do not steal, Do not bear false witness, Do not defraud, Honor your father and mother.' " And the man said to Jesus, "Teacher, all these I have observed from my youth." And Jesus looking upon him loved him, and said to him, "You lack one thing; go, sell what you have, and give to the poor, and you will have treasure in heaven; and come, follow me." At that saying his countenance fell, and he went away sorrowful; for he had great possessions.

And Jesus looked around and said to his disciples, "How hard it will be for those who have riches to enter the dominion of God!" And the disciples were amazed at his words. But Jesus said to them again, "Children, how hard it is to enter the dominion of God! It is easier for a camel to go through the eye of a needle than for the rich to enter the dominion of God." And they were exceedingly astonished, and said to him, "Then who can be saved?" [27]Jesus looked at them and said, "With humankind it is impossible, but not with God; for all things are possible with God."

FIRST READING

R Isaiah 53:10–11
E Isaiah 53:4–12
L Isaiah 53:10–12

⁴Surely he has borne our griefs
    and carried our sorrows;
yet we esteemed him stricken,
    smitten by God, and afflicted.
But he was wounded for our transgressions,
    and was bruised for our iniquities;
the chastisement that made us whole was upon him,
    by whose stripes we are healed.
All we like sheep have gone astray;
    we have turned each one to our own way,
and the LORD has laid on this servant
    the iniquity of us all.
This servant was oppressed and was afflicted,
    yet opened not his mouth;
like a lamb that is led to the slaughter,
    and like a ewe that before her shearers is dumb,
    so he opened not his mouth.
By oppression and judgment the servant was taken away;
    and as for his generation, who considered
that he was cut off out of the land of the living,
    stricken for the transgression of my people?
He was given a grave with the wicked,
    and was with the rich in death,
although having done no violence,
    having never spoken deceit.
¹⁰Yet it was the will of the LORD to bruise this servant;
    the LORD has put him to grief;
making himself an offering for sin,
    the servant shall see offspring and shall prolong his days;

the will of the LORD shall prosper in the hand of the servant,
¹¹who shall see the fruit of the travail of his soul and be
    satisfied;
by his knowledge shall the righteous one, my servant,
  make many to be accounted righteous;
  my servant shall bear their iniquities.
¹²Therefore I will divide a portion with the great for my servant
  who shall divide the spoil with the strong;
because my servant poured out his soul to death,
  and was numbered with the transgressors;
yet he bore the sin of many,
  and made intercession for the transgressors.

SECOND READING

R Hebrews 4:14–16
E Hebrews 4:12–16
L Hebrews 4:9–16

⁹There remains a sabbath rest for the people of God; for those who enter God's rest also cease from their labors just as God did.

Let us therefore strive to enter that rest, that no one fall by the same sort of disobedience. ¹²For the word of God is living and active, sharper than any two-edged sword, piercing to the division of soul and spirit, of joints and marrow, and discerning the thoughts and intentions of the heart. And before God no creature is hidden, but all are open and laid bare to the eyes of the one with whom we have to do.

¹⁴Since then we have a great high priest who has passed through the heavens, Jesus, the Son of God, let us hold fast our confession. For we have not a high priest who is unable to sympathize with our weaknesses, but one who in every respect has been tempted as we are, yet without sin. ¹⁶Let us then with confidence draw near to the throne of grace, that we may receive mercy and find grace to help in time of need.

226 TWENTY-NINTH SUNDAY IN ORDINARY TIME R
PROPER 24 E
TWENTY-SECOND SUNDAY AFTER PENTECOST L

GOSPEL

R Mark 10:42–45
E L Mark 10:35–45

[35]James and John, the sons of Zebedee, came forward to Jesus, saying, "Teacher, we want you to do for us whatever we ask of you." And Jesus said to them, "What do you want me to do for you?" And they said to him, "Grant us to sit, one at your right hand and one at your left, in your glory." But Jesus said to them, "You do not know what you are asking. Are you able to drink the cup that I drink, or to be baptized with the baptism with which I am baptized?" And they said to him, "We are able." And Jesus said to them, "The cup that I drink you will drink; and with the baptism with which I am baptized, you will be baptized; but to sit at my right hand or at my left is not mine to grant, but it is for those for whom it has been prepared." And when the ten heard it, they began to be indignant at James and John. [42]And Jesus called them to him and said to them, "You know that those who are supposed to rule over the Gentiles are domineering, and their mighty ones exercise authority over them. But it shall not be so among you; but whoever would be great among you must be your servant, and whoever would be first among you must be slave of all. [45]For the Man of Heaven also came not to be served but to serve, and to give his life as a ransom for many."

R THIRTIETH SUNDAY IN ORDINARY TIME
E PROPER 25
L TWENTY-THIRD SUNDAY AFTER PENTECOST

FIRST READING

R L Jeremiah 31:7–9

⁷For thus says the LORD:
"Sing aloud with gladness for Jacob,
    and raise shouts for the chief of the nations;
proclaim, give praise, and say,
    'The LORD has saved the remnant of Israel, the people of the
        LORD.'
Behold, I will bring them from the north country,
    and gather them from the farthest parts of the earth,
among them the blind and the lame,
    the woman with child and her who is in labor, together;
    a great company, they shall return here.
⁹With weeping they shall come,
    and with consolations I will lead them back,
I will make them walk by brooks of water,
    in a straight path in which they shall not stumble;
for I am as a father to Israel,
    and Ephraim is as my first-born."

E Isaiah 59:9–19

⁹Justice is far from us,
    and righteousness does not overtake us;
we look for light, and behold, darkness,
    and for brightness, but we walk in gloom.
We grope for the wall like the blind,
    we grope like those who have no eyes;
we stumble at noon as in the twilight,
    among those in full vigor we are like the dead.
We all growl like bears,
    we moan and moan like doves;
we look for justice, but there is none;
    for salvation, but it is far from us.

For our transgressions are multiplied before you,
    and our sins testify against us;
for our transgressions are with us,
    and we know our iniquities:
transgressing, and denying the LORD,
    and turning away from following our God,
speaking oppression and revolt,
    conceiving and uttering from the heart lying words.
Justice is turned back,
    and righteousness stands afar off;
for truth has fallen in the public squares,
    and uprightness cannot enter.
Truth is lacking,
    and the one who departs from evil is despoiled.
The LORD saw it and was displeased
    that there was no justice.
The LORD saw that there was nobody,
    and wondered that there was no one to intervene;
then the arm of the LORD brought victory,
    and the righteousness of God gave support.
The LORD put on righteousness as a breastplate,
    and donned a helmet of salvation;
the LORD, enwrapped in fury as a mantle,
    put on garments of vengeance for clothing.
According to their deeds, so will the LORD repay,
    wrath to God's adversaries, requital to God's enemies;
    to the coastlands the LORD will render requital.
[19]So they shall fear the name of the LORD from the west,
    and the glory of the LORD from the rising of the sun;
for the LORD will come like a rushing stream,
    which the wind of the LORD drives.

SECOND READING

R   Hebrews 5:1–6
L   Hebrews 5:1–10

[1]Every high priest chosen from among the people is appointed
to act on behalf of the people in relation to God, to offer gifts
and sacrifices for sins. The high priest can deal gently with the

ignorant and wayward, since he himself is beset with weakness. Because of this he is bound to offer sacrifice for his own sins as well as for those of the people. And one does not take the honor upon himself, but is called by God, just as Aaron was.

So also Christ did not exalt himself to be made a high priest, but was appointed by the one who said to him,

"You are my Son,
today I have begotten you";

[6]as God says also in another place,

"You are a priest for ever,
after the order of Melchizedek."

[7]In the days of his flesh, Jesus offered up prayers and supplications, with loud cries and tears, to the one who was able to save him from death, and for being God-fearing Jesus was heard. Although being a Son, Jesus learned obedience through what he suffered, and being made perfect Jesus became the source of eternal salvation to all who obey him, [10]being designated by God a high priest after the order of Melchizedek.

E   Hebrews 5:12–6:1, 9–12

[12]Although by this time you ought to be teachers, you need some one to teach you again the first principles of God's word. You need milk, not solid food; for every one who lives on milk is unskilled in the word of righteousness, being a child. But solid food is for the mature, for those who have their faculties trained by practice to distinguish good from evil.

[1]Therefore let us leave the elementary doctrine of Christ and go on to maturity, not laying again a foundation of repentance from dead works and of faith toward God.

[9]Though we speak thus, yet in your case, beloved, we feel sure of better things that belong to salvation. For God is not so unjust as to overlook your work and the love which you showed for the sake of God's name in serving the saints, as you still do. And we desire each one of you to show the same earnestness

in realizing the full assurance of hope until the end, [12]so that you may not be sluggish, but imitators of those who through faith and patience inherit the promises.

GOSPEL

R E L   Mark 10:46–52

[46]Jesus and his disciples came to Jericho; and as he was leaving Jericho with his disciples and a great multitude, Bartimaeus, a blind beggar, the son of Timaeus, was sitting by the roadside. And hearing that it was Jesus of Nazareth, he began to cry out and say, "Jesus, Son of David, have mercy on me!" And many rebuked him, telling him to be silent; but he cried out all the more, "Son of David, have mercy on me!" And Jesus stopped and said, "Call him." And they called the blind man, saying to him, "Take heart; rise, he is calling you." And throwing off his mantle he sprang up and came to Jesus. And Jesus said to him, "What do you want me to do for you?" And the blind man said to him, "Rabbi, let me receive my sight." [52]And Jesus said to him, "Go your way; your faith has made you well." And immediately he received his sight and followed Jesus on the way.

R **THIRTY-FIRST SUNDAY IN ORDINARY TIME**
E **PROPER 26**
L **TWENTY-FOURTH SUNDAY AFTER PENTECOST**

FIRST READING

R Deuteronomy 6:2–6
E L Deuteronomy 6:1–9

[Moses said to the people,]

¹"This is the commandment, the statutes and the ordinances which the LORD your God commanded me to teach you, that you may do them in the land to which you are going over, to possess it; ²that you may fear the LORD your God, you and your children and your children's children, by keeping all the statutes and the commandments of the LORD, which I command you, all the days of your life; and that your days may be prolonged. Hear therefore, O Israel, and be careful to do them; that it may go well with you, and that you may multiply greatly, as the LORD, the God of your forebears, has promised you, in a land flowing with milk and honey.

"Hear, O Israel: the LORD our God is one LORD; and you shall love the LORD your God with all your heart, and with all your soul, and with all your might. ⁶And these words which I command you this day shall be upon your heart; ⁷and you shall teach them diligently to your children, and shall talk of them when you sit in your house, and when you walk by the way, and when you lie down, and when you rise. And you shall bind them as a sign upon your hand, and they shall be as frontlets between your eyes. ⁹And you shall write them on the doorposts of your house and on your gates."

SECOND READING

R E L Hebrews 7:23–28

²³The former priests were many in number, because they were prevented by death from continuing in office; but Jesus holds his priesthood permanently, because he continues for ever. Con-

sequently he is able for all time to save those who draw near to God through him, living always to make intercession for them.

For it was fitting that we should have such a high priest, holy, blameless, unstained, separated from sinners, exalted above the heavens, who has no need, like those high priests, to offer sacrifices daily, first for his own sins and then for those of the people; he did this once for all when he offered up himself. [28]Indeed, the law appoints as high priests weak human beings, but the word of the oath, which came later than the law, appoints a Son who has been made perfect for ever.

GOSPEL

R   Mark 12:28b–34
E L   Mark 12:28–34

[28a]One of the scribes came up and heard the Sadducees disputing with one another, and seeing that Jesus answered them well, [28b]asked him, "Which commandment is the first of all?" Jesus answered, "The first is, 'Hear, O Israel: The Lord our God, the Lord is one; and you shall love the Lord your God with all your heart, and with all your soul, and with all your mind, and with all your strength.' The second is this, 'You shall love your neighbor as yourself.' There is no other commandment greater than these." And the scribe said to Jesus, "You are right, Teacher; you have truly said that God is one, and there is no other but God; and to love God with all the heart, and with all the understanding, and with all the strength, and to love one's neighbor as oneself, is much more than all whole burnt offerings and sacrifices." [34]And seeing that the scribe had answered wisely, Jesus said to him, "You are not far from the dominion of God." And after that no one dared to ask him any question.

R **THIRTY-SECOND SUNDAY IN ORDINARY TIME**
E **PROPER 27**
L **TWENTY-FIFTH SUNDAY AFTER PENTECOST**

FIRST READING

R 1 Kings 17:10–16
E L 1 Kings 17:8–16

⁸The word of the LORD came to Elijah, "Arise, go to Zarephath, which belongs to Sidon, and dwell there. Behold, I have commanded a widow there to feed you." ¹⁰So Elijah arose and went to Zarephath; and when he came to the gate of the city, behold, a widow was there gathering sticks; and he called to her and said, "Bring me a little water in a vessel, that I may drink." And as she was going to bring it, he called to her and said, "Bring me a morsel of bread in your hand." And she said, "As the LORD your God lives, I have nothing baked, only a handful of meal in a jar, and a little oil in a cruse; and now, I am gathering a couple of sticks, that I may go in and prepare it for myself and my son, that we may eat it, and die." And Elijah said to her, "Fear not; go and do as you have said; but first make me a little cake of it and bring it to me, and afterward make for yourself and your son. For thus says the LORD the God of Israel, 'The jar of meal shall not be spent, and the cruse of oil shall not fail, until the day that the LORD sends rain upon the earth.' " And she went and did as Elijah said; and she, and he, and her household ate for many days. ¹⁶The jar of meal was not spent, neither did the cruse of oil fail, according to the word of the LORD which the LORD spoke by Elijah.

SECOND READING

R E L Hebrews 9:24–28

²⁴Christ has entered, not into a sanctuary made with hands, a copy of the true one, but into heaven itself, now to appear in the presence of God on our behalf. Nor was it to offer himself repeatedly, as the high priest enters the Holy Place yearly with blood not his own; for then he would have had to suffer repeatedly since the foundation of the world. But as it is, Christ has

appeared once for all at the end of the age to put away sin by the sacrifice of himself. And just as it is appointed for human beings to die once, and after that comes judgment, [28]so Christ, having been offered once to bear the sins of many, will appear a second time, not to deal with sin but to save those who are eagerly waiting for him.

GOSPEL

R L   Mark 12:41–44
   E   Mark 12:38–44

[38]In his teaching Jesus said, "Beware of the scribes, who like to go about in long robes, and to have salutations in the market places and the best seats in the synagogues and the places of honor at feasts, who devour widows' houses and for a pretense make long prayers. They will receive the greater condemnation."

[41]And Jesus sat down opposite the treasury, and watched the multitude putting money into the treasury. Many rich people put in large sums. And a poor widow came, and put in two copper coins, which make a penny. And Jesus summoned his disciples, and said to them, "Truly, I say to you, this poor widow has put in more than all those who are contributing to the treasury. [44]For they all contributed out of their abundance; but she out of her poverty has put in everything she had, her whole living."

R THIRTY-THIRD SUNDAY IN ORDINARY TIME
E PROPER 28
L TWENTY-SIXTH SUNDAY AFTER PENTECOST

FIRST READING

R L Daniel 12:1–3
  E Daniel 12:1–4a

¹At that time shall arise Michael, the great ruler who has charge of your people. And there shall be a time of trouble, such as never has been since there was a nation till that time; but at that time your people shall be delivered, every one whose name shall be found written in the book. And many of those who sleep in the dust of the earth shall awake, some to everlasting life, and some to shame and everlasting contempt. ³And those who are wise shall shine like the brightness of the firmament; and those who turn many to righteousness, like the stars for ever and ever. ⁴ᵃBut you, Daniel, shut up the words, and seal the book, until the time of the end.

SECOND READING

R Hebrews 10:11–14, 18
L Hebrews 10:11–18

¹¹And every priest stands at the daily service, offering repeatedly the same sacrifices, which can never take away sins. But when Christ had offered for all time a single sacrifice for sins, he sat down at the right hand of God, then to wait until his enemies should be made a stool for his feet. ¹⁴For by a single offering Christ has perfected for all time those who are sanctified. ¹⁵And the Holy Spirit also bears witness to us; for after saying,

"This is the covenant that I will make with them
after those days, says the Lord:
I will put my laws on their hearts, and write them on their
  minds,"

then is added,

"I will remember their sins and their misdeeds no more."

¹⁸Where there is forgiveness of these, there is no longer any offering for sin.

E   Hebrews 10:31–39

³¹It is a fearful thing to fall into the hands of the living God.

But recall the former days when, after you were enlightened, you endured a hard struggle with sufferings, sometimes being publicly exposed to abuse and affliction, and sometimes being partners with those so treated. For you had compassion on the prisoners, and you joyfully accepted the plundering of your property, since you knew that you yourselves had a better possession and an abiding one. Therefore do not throw away your confidence, which has a great reward. For you have need of endurance, so that you may do the will of God and receive what is promised.

"For yet a little while,
and the coming one shall come and shall not tarry;
but my righteous ones shall live by faith,
and if they shrink back,
my soul has no pleasure in them."

³⁹But we are not of those who shrink back and are destroyed, but of those who have faith and keep their souls.

GOSPEL

R   Mark 13:24–32

[At that time Jesus said,]

²⁴"In those days, after that tribulation, the sun will be darkened, and the moon will not give its light, and the stars will be falling from heaven, and the powers in the heavens will be shaken. And then they will see the Man of Heaven coming in clouds with great power and glory. And then he will send out the angels, and gather his elect from the four winds, from the ends of the earth to the ends of heaven.

"From the fig tree learn its lesson: as soon as its branch becomes tender and puts forth its leaves, you know that summer is near. So also, when you see these things taking place, you know that he is near, at the very gates. Truly, I say to you, this generation will not pass away before all these things take place. Heaven and earth will pass away, but my words will not pass away.

³²"But of that day or that hour no one knows, not even the angels in heaven, nor the Son, but only the Father."

E Mark 13:14–23

[At that time Jesus said,]

¹⁴"When you see the desolating sacrilege set up where it ought not to be (let the reader understand), then let those who are in Judea flee to the mountains; let the one who is on the housetop not go down, nor enter the house, to take anything away; and let the one who is in the field not turn back to get a mantle. And alas for those who are with child and for those who are breastfeeding in those days! Pray that it may not happen in winter. For in those days there will be such tribulation as has not been from the beginning of the creation which God created until now, and never will be. And if the Lord had not shortened the days, no human being would be saved; but for the sake of the elect, the chosen ones, God shortened the days. And then if any one says to you, 'Look, here is the Christ!' or 'Look, there he is!' do not believe it. False Christs and false prophets will arise and show signs and wonders, to lead astray, if possible, the elect. ²³But take heed; I have told you all things beforehand."

L Mark 13:1–13

¹As Jesus came out of the temple, one of this disciples said to him, "Look, Teacher, what wonderful stones and what wonderful buildings!" And Jesus said to him, "Do you see these great buildings? There will not be left here one stone upon another, that will not be thrown down."

And as Jesus sat on the Mount of Olives opposite the temple, Peter and James and John and Andrew asked him privately, "Tell us, when will this be, and what will be the sign when these things are all to be accomplished?" And Jesus began to say to them, "Take heed that no one leads you astray. Many will come in my name, saying, 'I am the one!' and they will lead many astray. And when you hear of wars and rumors of wars, do not be alarmed; this must take place, but the end is not yet. For nation will rise against nation, and realm against realm; there will be earthquakes in various places, there will be famines; this is but the beginning of the birth-pangs.

"But take heed to yourselves; for they will deliver you up to councils; and you will be beaten in synagogues; and you will stand before governors and rulers for my sake, to bear testimony before them. And the gospel must first be preached to all nations. And when they bring you to trial and deliver you up, do not be anxious beforehand what you are to say; but say whatever is given you in that hour, for it is not you who speak, but the Holy Spirit. And brothers and sisters will deliver up one another to death, and the parent the child, and children will rise against parents and have them put to death; [13]and you will be hated by all for my name's sake. But the one who endures to the end will be saved."

L TWENTY-SEVENTH SUNDAY AFTER PENTECOST

FIRST READING

L Daniel 7:9–10

⁹As I looked,
   thrones were placed
      and one that was ancient of days sat down,
   whose raiment was white as snow,
      and the hair of whose head like pure wool,
   whose throne was fiery flames,
      its wheels were burning fire.
¹⁰A stream of fire issued
      and came forth from before the Ancient of Days,
   whom a thousand thousands served,
      and before whom ten thousand times ten thousand stood;
   the court sat in judgment,
      and the books were opened.

SECOND READING

L Hebrews 13:20–21

²⁰May the God of peace who brought again from the dead our
Lord Jesus, the great shepherd of the sheep, by the blood of
the eternal covenant, ²¹equip you with everything good that
you may do God's will, working in you that which is pleasing
in the sight of God, through Jesus Christ; to whom be glory for
ever and ever. Amen.

GOSPEL

L Mark 13:24–31

[At that time Jesus said,]

²⁴"In those days, after that tribulation, the sun will be dark-
ened, and the moon will not give its light, and the stars will be
falling from heaven, and the powers in the heavens will be
shaken. And then they will see the Man of Heaven coming in
clouds with great power and glory. And then he will send out

the angels, and gather his elect from the four winds, from the ends of the earth to the ends of heaven.

"From the fig tree learn its lesson: as soon as its branch becomes tender and puts forth its leaves, you know that summer is near. So also, when you see these things taking place, you know that he is near, at the very gates. Truly, I say to you, this generation will not pass away before all these things take place. [31]Heaven and earth will pass away, but my words will not pass away."

R LAST SUNDAY IN ORDINARY TIME, CHRIST THE KING

E PROPER 29

L CHRIST THE KING, LAST SUNDAY AFTER PENTECOST

FIRST READING

R L   Daniel 7:13–14
   E   Daniel 7:9–14

⁹As I looked,
  thrones were placed
    and one that was ancient of days sat down,
  whose raiment was white as snow,
    and the hair of whose head like pure wool,
  whose throne was fiery flames,
    its wheels were burning fire.
  A stream of fire issued
    and came forth from before the Ancient of Days,
  whom a thousand thousands served,
    and before whom ten thousand times ten thousand stood;
  the court sat in judgment,
    and the books were opened.

I looked then because of the sound of the great words which the horn was speaking. And as I looked, the beast was slain, and its body destroyed and given over to be burned with fire. As for the rest of the beasts, their dominion was taken away, but their lives were prolonged for a season and a time.

¹³I saw in the night visions,
and behold, with the clouds of heaven
  there came one like a human being,
and he came before the Ancient of Days,
  before whom he was presented.
¹⁴And to the human being, was given rule
  and glory and dominion,
that all peoples, nations, and languages
  should serve him;

the rule of this man of heaven is an everlasting rule,
   which shall not pass away,
and his dominion one
   that shall not be destroyed.

SECOND READING

R   Revelation 1:5–8
E   Revelation 1:1–8
L   Revelation 1:4b–8

[1]The revelation of Jesus Christ, which God gave Jesus to show to the servants of God what must soon take place; and Jesus made it known by sending an angel to John, the servant of God, who bore witness to the word of God and to the testimony of Jesus Christ, even to all that he saw. Blessed is the one who reads aloud the words of the prophecy, and blessed are those who hear, and who keep what is written therein; for the time is near.

John to the seven churches that are in Asia:

[4b]Grace to you and peace from the one who is and who was and who is to come, and from the seven spirits who are before God's throne, [5]and from Jesus Christ the faithful witness, the first-born of the dead, and the ruler of rulers on earth.

To the one who loves us and has freed us from our sins by his blood and made us a dominion, priests to his God and Father, to Jesus Christ be glory and dominion for ever and ever. Amen. Behold, he is coming with the clouds, and every eye will see him, every one who pierced him; and all tribes of the earth will wail on account of him. Even so. Amen.

[8]"I am the Alpha and the Omega," says the Lord God, who is and who was and who is to come, the Almighty.

GOSPEL

R John 18:33b–37
E L John 18:33–37

[33a]Pilate entered the praetorium again and called Jesus, [33b]and said to him, "Are you the King of the Jews?" Jesus answered, "Do you say this of your own accord, or did others say it to you about me?" Pilate answered, "Am I a Jew? Your own nation and the chief priests have handed you over to me; what have you done?" Jesus answered, "My kingship is not of this world; if my kingship were of this world, my servants would fight, that I might not be handed over to the Judeans; but my kingship is not from this world." [37]Pilate said to him, "So you are a king?" Jesus answered, "You say that I am a king. For this I was born, and for this I have come into the world, to bear witness to the truth. Every one who is of the truth hears my voice."

March 25

R E L ANNUNCIATION OF OUR LORD

FIRST READING

R E L Isaiah 7:10–14

¹⁰Again the LORD spoke to Ahaz, "Ask a sign of the LORD your God; let it be deep as Sheol or high as heaven." But Ahaz said, "I will not ask, and I will not put the LORD to the test." And the LORD said, "Hear then, O house of David! Is it too little for you to weary humankind, that you weary my God also? ¹⁴Therefore this very Lord will give you a sign. Behold, a young woman shall conceive and bear a son, and shall call his name Immanuel."

SECOND READING

R Hebrews 10:4–10
E Hebrews 10:5–10

⁴It is impossible that the blood of bulls and goats should take away sins.

⁵Consequently, coming into the world, Christ said,

"Sacrifices and offerings you have not desired,
but a body you have prepared for me;
in burnt offerings and sin offerings you have taken no pleasure.
Then I said, 'Lo, I have come to do your will, O God,'
as it is written of me in the roll of the book."

When Christ said above, "You have neither desired nor taken pleasure in sacrifices and offerings and burnt offerings and sin offerings" (these are offered according to the law), then Christ added, "Lo, I have come to do your will." Christ abolishes the first in order to establish the second. ¹⁰And by that will we have been sanctified through the offering of the body of Jesus Christ once for all.

L   1 Timothy 3:16

¹⁶Great indeed, we confess, is the mystery of our religion:

He was manifested in the flesh,
vindicated in the Spirit,
    seen by angels,
preached among the nations,
believed on in the world,
    taken up in glory.

GOSPEL

R E L   Luke 1:26–38

²⁶In the sixth month the angel Gabriel was sent from God to a city of Galilee named Nazareth, to a virgin betrothed to a man whose name was Joseph, of the house of David; and the virgin's name was Mary. And the angel came to her and said, "Hail, O favored one, the Lord is with you!" But she was greatly troubled at the saying, and considered in her mind what sort of greeting this might be. And the angel said to her, "Do not be afraid, Mary, for you have found favor with God. And behold, you will conceive in your womb and bear a son, and you shall call his name Jesus.

"He will be great, and will be called the Son of the Most High; and the Lord God will give to him the throne of his forebear
    David,
and he will reign over the house of Jacob for ever;
and of his dominion there will be no end."

And Mary said to the angel, "How can this be, since I am a
    virgin?" And the angel said to her,

"The Holy Spirit will come upon you,
and the power of the Most High will overshadow you;
therefore the child to be born will be called holy,
the Son of God.

"And behold, your kinswoman Elizabeth in her old age has also conceived a son; and this is the sixth month with her who was called barren. For with God nothing will be impossible." [38]And Mary said, "Behold, I am the serving maid of the Lord; let it be to me according to your word." And the angel departed from her.

R E L THE VISITATION

FIRST READING

R E   Zephaniah 3:14–18a

> [14]Sing aloud, O daughter Zion;
>   shout, O Israel!
> Rejoice and exult with all your heart,
>   O daughter Jerusalem!
> The LORD has taken away the judgments against you,
>   and has cast out your enemies.
> The LORD, the Sovereign of Israel, is in your midst;
>   you shall fear evil no more.
> On that day it shall be said to Jerusalem:
> "Do not fear, O Zion;
>   let not your hands grow weak.
> The LORD, your God, is in your midst,
>   a mighty one who gives victory;
> the LORD will rejoice over you with gladness,
>   and will renew you in love;
> the LORD will exult over you with loud singing
>   [18a]as on a day of festival."

L   Isaiah 11:1–5

> [1]There shall come forth a shoot from the stump of Jesse,
>   and a branch shall grow out of its roots.
> Upon this one the Spirit of the LORD shall rest,
>   the spirit of wisdom and understanding,
>   the spirit of counsel and might,
>   the spirit of knowledge and the fear of the LORD.
> And his delight shall be in the fear of the LORD.
> He shall not judge by what the eyes see,
>   or decide by what the ears hear;
> but with righteousness he shall judge the poor,
>   and decide with equity for the meek of the earth;
> and he shall smite the earth with the rod of his mouth,
>   and with the breath of his lips shall slay the wicked.

[5]Righteousness shall be the belt of his waist,
    and faithfulness shall gird his loins.

SECOND READING

R   Romans 12:9–16b
L   Romans 12:9–16

[9]Let love be genuine; hate what is evil, hold fast to what is good; love one another with familial affection; outdo one another in showing honor. Never flag in zeal, be aglow with the Spirit, serve the Lord. Rejoice in your hope, be patient in tribulation, be constant in prayer. Contribute to the needs of the saints, practice hospitality.

Bless those who persecute you; bless and do not curse them. Rejoice with those who rejoice, weep with those who weep. [16a]Live in harmony with one another; [16b]do not be haughty, but associate with the lowly; [16c]never be conceited.

E   Colossians 3:12–17

[12]Put on then, as God's chosen ones, holy and beloved, compassion, kindness, lowliness, meekness, and patience, forbearing one another and, if one has a complaint against another, forgiving each other; as the Lord has forgiven you, so you also must forgive. And above all these put on love, which binds everything together in perfect harmony. And let the peace of Christ rule in your hearts, to which indeed you were called in the one body. And be thankful. Let the word of Christ dwell in you richly, teach and admonish one another in all wisdom, and sing psalms and hymns and spiritual songs with thankfulness in your hearts of God. [17]And whatever you do, in word or deed, do everything in the name of the Lord Jesus, giving thanks to God, the Father, through him.

GOSPEL

R Luke 1:39–56
E Luke 1:39–49
L Luke 1:39–47

[39]In those days Mary arose and went with haste into the hill country, to a city of Judah, and she entered the house of Zechariah and greeted Elizabeth. And when Elizabeth heard the greeting of Mary, the baby leaped in her womb; and Elizabeth was filled with the Holy Spirit and she exclaimed with a loud cry, "Blessed are you among women, and blessed is the fruit of your womb! And why is this granted me, that the mother of my Lord should come to me? For behold, when the voice of your greeting came to my ears, the baby in my womb leaped for joy. And blessed is she who believed that there would be a fulfillment of what was spoken to her from the Lord." And Mary said,

"My soul magnifies the Lord,
[47]and my spirit rejoices in God my Savior
[48]who has looked with favor on me, a lowly serving maid.
From this day all generations will call me blessed.
[49]The Mighty One has done great things for me;
holy the name of the Lord,
[50]whose mercy is on the God-fearing
from generation to generation.
The arm of the Lord is filled with strength,
scattering the proudhearted.
God cast the mighty from their thrones,
lifting up the lowly.
God filled the hungry with good things,
sending the rich away empty.
God has come to the help of Israel, the Lord's servant,
remembering mercy,
the mercy promised to our forebears,
to Abraham and his children forever."

[56]And Mary remained with her about three months, and returned to her home.

R E TRANSFIGURATION

FIRST READING

R Daniel 7:9–10, 13–14

⁹As I looked,
  thrones were placed
    and one that was ancient of days sat down,
  whose raiment was white as snow,
    and the hair of whose head like pure wool,
  whose throne was fiery flames,
    its wheels were burning fire.
¹⁰A stream of fire issued
    and came forth from before the Ancient of Days,
  whom a thousand thousands served,
    and before whom ten thousand times ten thousand stood;
  the court sat in judgment,
    and the books were opened.
¹³I saw in the night visions,
  and behold, with the clouds of heaven
    there came one like a human being,
  and he came before the Ancient of Days,
    before whom he was presented.
¹⁴And to the human being was given rule
    and glory and dominion,
  that all peoples, nations, and languages
    should serve him;
  the rule of this man of heaven is an everlasting rule,
    which shall not pass away,
  and his dominion one
    that shall not be destroyed.

E Exodus 34:29–35

²⁹When Moses came down from Mount Sinai, with the two
tables of the testimony in his hand as he came down from the
mountain, Moses did not know that the skin of his face shone
because he had been talking with God. And when Aaron and

all the people of Israel saw Moses, behold, the skin of his face shone, and they were afraid to come near him. But Moses called to them; and Aaron and all the leaders of the congregation returned to him, and Moses talked with them. And afterward all the people of Israel came near, and Moses gave them in commandment all that the LORD had spoken with him in Mount Sinai. And when Moses had finished speaking with them, he put a veil on his face; but whenever Moses went in before the LORD to speak with the LORD, Moses took the veil off, until he came out; and when he came out, and told the people of Israel what he was commanded, ³⁵the people of Israel saw the face of Moses, that the skin of Moses' face shone; and Moses would put the veil upon his face again, until he went in to speak with the LORD.

SECOND READING

R   2 Peter 1:16–19
E   2 Peter 1:13–21

¹³I think it right, as long as I am in this body, to stir you up by way of reminder, since I know that the putting off of my body will be soon, as our Lord Jesus Christ showed me. And I will see to it that after my departure you may be able at any time to recall these things.

¹⁶For we did not follow cleverly devised myths when we made known to you the power and coming of our Lord Jesus Christ, but we were eyewitnesses of his majesty. For when Jesus our Lord received honor and glory from God, the Father, and the voice was borne to him by the Majestic Glory, "This is my Son, my beloved one, with whom I am well pleased," we heard this voice borne from heaven, for we were with Jesus on the holy mountain. ¹⁹And we have the prophetic word made more sure. You will do well to pay attention to this as to a lamp shining in a dark place, until the day dawns and the morning star rises in your hearts. ²⁰First of all you must understand this, that no prophecy of scripture is a matter of one's own interpretation, ²¹because no prophecy ever came by human impulse, but people moved by the Holy Spirit spoke from God.

GOSPEL

R   Mark 9:2–10

²After six days Jesus took with him Peter and James and John, and led them up a high mountain apart by themselves; and he was transfigured before them, and his garments became glistening, intensely white, as no fuller on earth could bleach them. And there appeared to them Elijah with Moses; and they were talking to Jesus. And Peter said to Jesus, "Rabbi, it is well that we are here; let us make three booths, one for you and one for Moses and one for Elijah." For he did not know what to say, for they were exceedingly afraid. And a cloud overshadowed them, and a voice came out of the cloud, "This is my Son, the beloved one; listen to him." And suddenly looking around they no longer saw any one with them but Jesus only.

And as they were coming down the mountain, Jesus charged them to tell no one what they had seen, until the Man of Heaven should have risen from the dead. ¹⁰So they kept the matter to themselves, questioning what the rising from the dead meant.

E   Luke 9:28–36

²⁸About eight days after these sayings Jesus took with him Peter and John and James, and went up on the mountain to pray. And as he was praying, the appearance of his countenance was altered, and his raiment became dazzling white. And behold, two men talked with him, Moses and Elijah, who appeared in glory and spoke of his departure, which he was to accomplish at Jerusalem. Now Peter and those who were with him were heavy with sleep, and when they wakened they saw his glory and the two men who stood with him. And as the men were parting from him, Peter said to Jesus, "Master, it is well that we are here; let us make three booths, one for you and one for Moses and one for Elijah"—not knowing what he said. As he said this, a cloud came and overshadowed them; and they were afraid as they entered the cloud. And a voice came out of the cloud, saying, "This is my Son, the chosen one; listen to him!" ³⁶And when the voice had spoken, Jesus was found alone. And they kept silence and told no one in those days anything of what they had seen.

September 29

R MICHAEL, GABRIEL, AND RAPHAEL
E L ST. MICHAEL AND ALL ANGELS

FIRST READING

R Daniel 7:9–10, 13–14

[9]As I looked,
 thrones were placed
  and one that was ancient of days sat down,
 whose raiment was white as snow,
  and the hair of whose head like pure wool,
 whose throne was fiery flames,
  its wheels were burning fire.
[10]A stream of fire issued
  and came forth from before the Ancient of Days,
 whom a thousand thousands served,
  and before whom ten thousand times ten thousand stood;
 the court sat in judgment,
  and the books were opened.
[13]I saw in the night visions,
 and behold, with the clouds of heaven
  there came one like a human being,
 and he came before the Ancient of Days,
  before whom he was presented.
[14]And to the human being was given rule
  and glory and dominion,
 that all peoples, nations, and languages
  should serve him;
 the rule of this man of heaven is an everlasting rule,
  which shall not pass away,
 and his dominion one
  that shall not be destroyed.

E Genesis 28:10–17

[10]Jacob left Beer-sheba, and went toward Haran. And he came
to a certain place, and stayed there that night, because the sun
had set. Taking one of the stones of the place, Jacob put it
under his head and lay down in that place to sleep. And he

dreamed that there was a ladder set up on the earth, and the top of it reached to heaven; and behold, the angels of God were ascending and descending on it! And behold, the LORD stood above it and said, "I am the LORD, the God of Abraham your father and the God of Isaac; the land on which you lie I will give to you and to your descendants; and your descendants shall be like the dust of the earth, and you shall spread abroad to the west and to the east and to the north and to the south; and by you and your descendants shall all the families of the earth bless themselves. Behold, I am with you and will keep you wherever you go, and will bring you back to this land; for I will not leave you until I have done that of which I have spoken to you." Then Jacob awoke from his sleep and said, "Surely the LORD is in this place; and I did not know it." ¹⁷And Jacob was afraid, and said, "How awesome is this place! This is none other than the house of God, and this is the gate of heaven."

L   Daniel 10:10–14; 12:1–3

¹⁰Behold, a hand touched me and set me trembling on my hands and knees. And a voice said to me, "O Daniel, man greatly beloved, give heed to the words that I speak to you, and stand upright, for now I have been sent to you." While these words were spoken to me, I stood up trembling. Then the voice said to me, "Fear not, Daniel, for from the first day that you set your mind to understand and humbled yourself before your God, your words have been heard, and I have come because of your words. The ruler of the realm of Persia withstood me twenty-one days; but Michael, one of the chief rulers, came to help me, so I left Michael there with the ruler of the realm of Persia ¹⁴and came to make you understand what is to befall your people in the latter days. For the vision is for days yet to come.

¹"At that time shall arise Michael, the great ruler who has charge of your people. And there shall be a time of trouble, such as never has been since there was a nation till that time; but at that time your people shall be delivered, every one whose name shall be found written in the book. And many of

those who sleep in the dust of the earth shall awake, some to everlasting life, and some to shame and everlasting contempt. [3]And those who are wise shall shine like the brightness of the firmament; and those who turn many to righteousness, like the stars for ever and ever."

SECOND READING

E L Revelation 12:7–12

[7]Now war arose in heaven, Michael and the angels fighting against the dragon; and the dragon and its angels fought, but they were defeated and there was no longer any place for them in heaven. And the great dragon was thrown down, that ancient serpent, who is called the Devil and Satan, the deceiver of the whole world—the dragon was thrown down to the earth, together with its angels. And I heard a loud voice in heaven, saying, "Now the salvation and the power and the dominion of our God and the authority of the Christ of God have come, for the accuser of our communities has been thrown down, who accuses them day and night before our God. And they have conquered the accuser by the blood of the Lamb and by the word of their testimony, for they loved not their lives even unto death. [12]Rejoice then, O heaven and you that dwell therein! But woe to you, O earth and sea, for the devil has come down to you in great wrath, knowing that its time is short."

GOSPEL

R E John 1:47–51

[47]Jesus saw Nathanael coming to him, and said of him, "Behold, an Israelite indeed, in whom is no guile!" Nathanael said to Jesus, "How do you know me?" Jesus answered him, "Before Philip called you, when you were under the fig tree, I saw you." Nathanael answered him, "Rabbi, you are the Son of God! You are the King of Israel!" Jesus answered him, "Because I said to you, I saw you under the fig tree, do you believe? You shall see greater things than these." [51]And Jesus said to him, "Truly, truly, I say to you, you will see heaven opened, and

the angels of God ascending and descending upon the Man of Heaven."

L   Luke 10:17–20

[17]The seventy disciples returned with joy, saying, "Lord, even the demons are subject to us in your name!" And Jesus said to them, "I saw Satan fall like lightning from heaven. Behold, I have given you authority to tread upon serpents and scorpions, and over all the power of the enemy; and nothing shall hurt you. [20]Nevertheless do not rejoice in this, that the spirits are subject to you; but rejoice that your names are written in heaven."

R E L ALL SAINTS

FIRST READING

R Revelation 7:2–4, 9–14

[2]I saw another angel ascend from the rising of the sun, with the seal of the living God, and the angel called with a loud voice to the four angels who had been given power to harm earth and sea, saying, "Do not harm the earth or the sea or the trees, till we have sealed the servants of our God upon their foreheads." [4]And I heard the number of the sealed, a hundred and forty-four thousand sealed, out of every tribe of the children of Israel.

[9]After this I looked, and behold, a great multitude which no one could number, from every nation, from all tribes and peoples and tongues, standing before the throne and before the Lamb, clothed in white robes, with palm branches in their hands, and crying out with a loud voice, "Salvation belongs to our God who sits upon the throne, and to the Lamb!" And all the angels stood round the throne and round the elders and the four living creatures, and they fell on their faces before the throne and worshiped God, saying, "Amen! Blessing and glory and wisdom and thanksgiving and honor and power and might be to our God for ever and ever! Amen."

Then one of the elders addressed me, saying, "Who are these, clothed in white robes, and whence have they come?" [14]I said to him, "Sir, you know." And he said to me, "These are they who have come out of the great tribulation; they have washed their robes and made them white in the blood of the Lamb."

E Sirach 44:1–10, 13–14 §

[1]Let us now praise famous men,
    and our fathers in their generations.
The Lord apportioned to them great glory,
    the majesty of the Lord from the beginning.
There were those who ruled in their realms,
    and were men renowned for their power,

giving counsel by their understanding,
  and proclaiming prophecies;
leaders of the people in their deliberations
  and in understanding of learning for the people,
  wise in their words of instruction;
those who composed musical tunes,
  and set forth verses in writing;
rich men furnished with resources,
  living peaceably in their habitations—
all these were honored in their generations,
  and were the glory of their times.
There are some of them who have left a name,
  so that their praise might be proclaimed.
And there are some who have no memorial,
  who have perished as though they had not lived;
they have become as though they had not been born,
  and so have their children after them.
¹⁰But these were men of mercy,
  whose righteous deeds have not been forgotten.
¹³Their posterity will continue for ever,
  and their glory will not be blotted out.
¹⁴Their bodies were buried in peace,
  and their name lives to all generations.

L   Isaiah 26:1–4, 8–9, 12–13, 19–21

¹In that day this song will be sung in the land of Judah:

"We have a strong city;
  the Lord sets up salvation
  as walls and bulwarks.
Open the gates,
  that the righteous nation which keeps faith
  may enter in.
You keep in perfect peace
  those whose mind is stayed on you,
  because they trust in you.
⁴Trust in the Lord for ever,
  for the Lord God
  is an everlasting rock.

⁸In the path of your judgments,
   O Lord, we wait for you;
your memorial name
   is the desire of our soul.
⁹My soul yearns for you in the night,
   my spirit within me earnestly seeks you.
¹²O Lord, you will ordain peace for us,
   you have wrought for us all our works.
¹³O Lord our God,
   other lords besides you have ruled over us,
   but your name alone we acknowledge.
¹⁹Your dead shall live, their bodies shall rise.
   O dwellers in the dust, awake and sing for joy!
For your dew is a dew of light,
   and on the land of the shades you will let it fall.
Come, my people, enter your chambers,
   and shut your doors behind you;
hide yourselves for a little while
   until the wrath is past.
²¹For behold, the Lord is coming forth from the holy place
   to punish the inhabitants of the earth for their iniquity,
and the earth will disclose the blood shed upon it,
   and will no more cover its slain."

SECOND READING

R   1 John 3:1–3

¹See what love the Father has given us, that we should be
called children of God; and so we are. The reason why the
world does not know us is that it did not know God. Beloved,
we are God's children now; it does not yet appear what we
shall be, but we know that when it appears we shall be like
God, for we shall see God as God is. ³And all who thus hope
in God purify themselves as the Son is pure.

E   Revelation 7:2–4, 9–17

²I saw another angel ascend from the rising of the sun, with
the seal of the living God, and the angel called with a loud
voice to the four angels who had been given power to harm

earth and sea, saying, "Do not harm the earth or the sea or the trees, till we have sealed the servants of our God upon their foreheads." [4]And I heard the number of the sealed, a hundred and forty-four thousand sealed, out of every tribe of the children of Israel.

[9]After this I looked, and behold, a great multitude which no one could number, from every nation, from all tribes and peoples and tongues, standing before the throne and before the Lamb, clothed in white robes, with palm branches in their hands, and crying out with a loud voice, "Salvation belongs to our God who sits upon the throne, and to the Lamb!" And all the angels stood round the throne and round the elders and the four living creatures, and they fell on their faces before the throne and worshiped God, saying, "Amen! Blessing and glory and wisdom and thanksgiving and honor and power and might be to our God for ever and ever! Amen."

Then one of the elders addressed me, saying, "Who are these, clothed in white robes, and whence have they come?" I said to him, "Sir, you know." And he said to me, "These are they who have come out of the great tribulation; they have washed their robes and made them white in the blood of the Lamb.

"Therefore are they before the throne of God,
   and serve God day and night within the temple;
   and the one who sits upon the throne will shelter them.
They shall hunger no more, neither thirst any more;
   the sun shall not strike them, nor any scorching heat.
[17]For the Lamb in the midst of the throne will be their
      shepherd,
   and will guide them to springs of living water;
and God will wipe away every tear from their eyes."

L   Revelation 21:9–11, 22–27

[9]Then came one of the seven angels who had the seven bowls full of the seven last plagues, and spoke to me, saying, "Come, I will show you the Bride, the wife of the Lamb." And in the Spirit the angel carried me away to a great, high mountain, and

showed me the holy city Jerusalem coming down out of heaven from God, [21]having the glory of God, its radiance like a most rare jewel, like a jasper, clear as crystal.

[22]And I saw no temple in the city, for its temple is the Lord God the Almighty and the Lamb. And the city has no need of sun or moon to shine upon it, for the glory of God is its light, and its lamp is the Lamb. By its light shall the nations walk; and the rulers of the earth shall bring their glory into it, and its gates shall never be shut by day—and there shall no night there; they shall bring into it the glory and the honor of the nations. [27]But nothing unclean shall enter it, nor any one who practices abomination or falsehood, but only those who are written in the Lamb's book of life.

GOSPEL

R Matthew 5:1–12a
E L Matthew 5:1–12

[1]Seeing the crowds, Jesus went up on the mountain and sat down, and his disciples came to him. And Jesus opened his mouth and taught them, saying:

"Blessed are the poor in spirit, for theirs is the dominion of heaven.

"Blessed are those who mourn, for they shall be comforted.

"Blessed are the meek, for they shall inherit the earth.

"Blessed are those who hunger and thirst for righteousness, for they shall be satisfied.

"Blessed are the merciful, for they shall obtain mercy.

"Blessed are the pure in heart, for they shall see God.

"Blessed are the peacemakers, for they shall be called children of God.

"Blessed are those who are persecuted for righteousness' sake, for theirs is the dominion of heaven.

"Blessed are you when you are reviled and persecuted and all kinds of evil is uttered against you falsely on my account. [12a]Rejoice and be glad, for your reward is great in heaven, [12b]for the prophets who were before you were persecuted in the same way."

R FOR THE UNITY OF ALL CHRISTIANS
E FOR THE UNITY OF THE CHURCH
L UNITY

FIRST READING

R Ezekiel 36:24–28

[Thus says the LORD:]

²⁴"I will take you from the nations, and gather you from all the countries, and bring you into your own land. I will sprinkle clean water upon you, and you shall be clean from all your uncleannesses, and from all your idols I will cleanse you. A new heart I will give you, and a new spirit I will put within you; and I will take out of your flesh the heart of stone and give you a heart of flesh. And I will put my spirit within you, and cause you to walk in my statutes and be careful to observe my ordinances. ²⁸You shall dwell in the land which I gave to your forebears; and you shall be my people, and I will be your God."

E Isaiah 35:1–10

¹The wilderness and the dry land shall be glad,
   the desert shall rejoice and blossom;
like the crocus it shall blossom abundantly,
   and rejoice with joy and singing.
The glory of Lebanon shall be given to it,
   the majesty of Carmel and Sharon.
They shall see the glory of the LORD,
   the majesty of our God.
Strengthen the weak hands,
   and make firm the feeble knees.
Say to those who are of a fearful heart,
   "Be strong, fear not!
Behold, your God
   will come with vengeance,
with the recompense of God.
   God will come and save you."
Then the eyes of the blind shall be opened,

264 FOR THE UNITY OF ALL CHRISTIANS R
FOR THE UNITY OF THE CHURCH E
UNITY L

and the ears of the deaf unstopped;
then shall the lame leap like a hart,
   and the tongue of the dumb sing for joy.
For the waters shall break forth in the wilderness,
   and streams in the desert;
the burning sand shall become a pool,
   and the thirsty ground springs of water;
the haunt of jackals shall become a swamp,
   the grass shall become reeds and rushes.
And a highway shall be there,
   and it shall be called the Holy Way;
the unclean shall not pass over it,
   and fools shall not err therein.
No lion shall be there,
   nor shall any ravenous beast come up on it;
they shall not be found there,
   but the redeemed shall walk there.
[10]And the ransomed of the Lord shall return,
   and come to Zion with singing;
   everlasting joy shall be upon their heads;
   they shall obtain joy and gladness,
   and sorrow and sighing shall flee away.

L   Isaiah 2:2–4

[2]It shall come to pass in the latter days
   that the mountain of the house of the Lord
shall be established as the highest of the mountains,
   and shall be raised above the hills;
and all the nations shall flow to it,
   and many peoples shall come, and say:
"Come, let us go up to the mountain of the Lord,
   to the house of Jacob's God,
who will teach us the ways of the Lord,
   that we may walk in the paths of God."
For out of Zion shall go forth the law,
   and the word of the Lord from Jerusalem.
[4]God shall judge between the nations,
   and shall decide for many peoples;
and they shall beat their swords into plowshares,

R   FOR THE UNITY OF ALL CHRISTIANS 265
E   FOR THE UNITY OF THE CHURCH
L   UNITY

and their spears into pruning hooks;
nation shall not lift up sword against nation,
    neither shall they learn war any more.

SECOND READING

R E L Ephesians 4:1–6

[1]I therefore, a prisoner for the Lord, beg you to lead a life worthy of the calling to which you have been called, with all lowliness and meekness, with patience, forbearing one another in love, eager to maintain the unity of the Spirit in the bond of peace. There is one body and one Spirit, just as you were called to the one hope that belongs to your call, one Lord, one faith, one baptism, [6]one God and Father of us all, who is above all and through all and in all.

GOSPEL

R John 17:20–26
E John 17:6a, 15–23
L John 17:15–23

[At that time Jesus said,]

[6a]"I have manifested your name to those whom you gave me out of the world. [15]I do not pray that you should take them out of the world, but that you should keep them from the evil one. They are not of the world, even as I am not of the world. Sanctify them in the truth; your word is truth. As you sent me into the world, so I have sent them into the world. And for their sake I consecrate myself, that they also may be consecrated in truth.

[20]"I do not pray for these only, but also for those who believe in me through their word, that they may all be one; even as you, Father, are in me, and I in you, that they also may be in us, so that the world may believe that you have sent me. The glory which you have given me I have given to them, that they may be one even as we are one, [23]I in them and you in me, that they may become perfectly one, so that the world may know that you have sent me and have loved them even as you

have loved me. ²⁴Father, I desire that they also, whom you have given me, may be with me where I am, to behold my glory which you have given me in your love for me before the foundation of the world. O righteous Father, the world has not known you, but I have known you; and these know that you have sent me. ²⁶I made known to them your name, and I will make it known, that the love with which you have loved me may be in them, and I in them."

SCRIPTURAL INDEX